6.95

my brother Sam is dead

my brother Sam is dead

*by James Lincoln Collier
and
Christopher Collier*

Four Winds Press
New York

Books by James Lincoln Collier

ROCK STAR

THE TEDDY BEAR HABIT

THE HARD LIFE OF THE TEENAGER

INSIDE JAZZ

WHY DOES EVERYBODY THINK I'M NUTTY?

Books by Christopher Collier

ROGER SHERMAN'S CONNECTICUT:
YANKEE POLITICS AND THE AMERICAN REVOLUTION

CONNECTICUT IN THE CONTINENTAL CONGRESS

LIBRARY OF CONGRESS CATALOGING IN PUBLICATION DATA
Collier, James Lincoln.
  My brother Sam is dead.
  SUMMARY: Recounts tragedy that strikes the Meeker family
during the Revolution when one son joins the rebel forces
while the rest of the family tries to stay neutral in a Tory
town.
  [1. United States—History—Revolution, 1775–1783—
Fiction] I. Collier, Christopher, joint author. II. Title.
PZ7.C678My   [Fic]   74–8350
ISBN 0–590–07339–7

PUBLISHED BY FOUR WINDS PRESS
A DIVISION OF SCHOLASTIC MAGAZINES, INC., NEW YORK, N.Y.
COPYRIGHT © 1974 BY JAMES LINCOLN COLLIER
AND CHRISTOPHER COLLIER
ALL RIGHTS RESERVED
PRINTED IN THE UNITED STATES OF AMERICA
LIBRARY OF CONGRESS CATALOG CARD NUMBER: 74–8350
3   4   5   78   77   76   75

For Sally and Ned, who live there

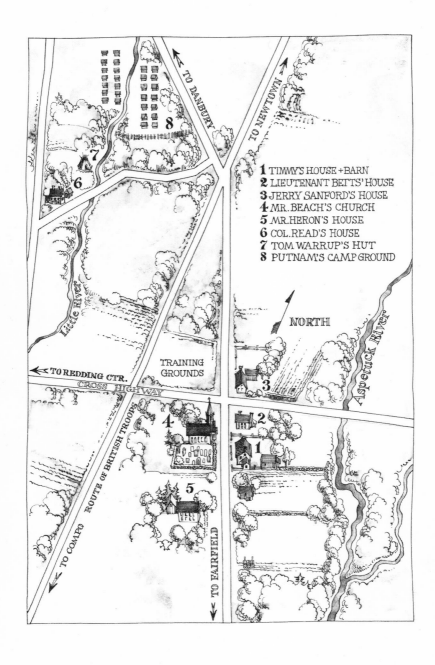

1 TIMMY'S HOUSE + BARN
2 LIEUTENANT BETTS' HOUSE
3 JERRY SANFORD'S HOUSE
4 MR. BEACH'S CHURCH
5 MR. HERON'S HOUSE
6 COL. READ'S HOUSE
7 TOM WARRUP'S HUT
8 PUTNAM'S CAMP GROUND

TO DANBURY

TO NEWTOWN

NORTH

Little River

Aspetuck River

TO REDDING CTR.
CROSS HIGHWAY

TRAINING GROUNDS

ROUTE OF BRITISH TROOPS

TO COMPO

TO FAIRFIELD

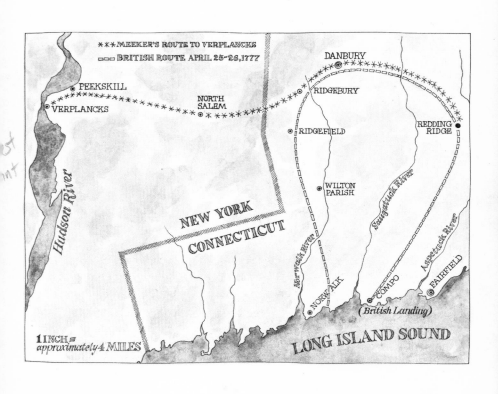

I

I<small>T WAS APRIL, AND OUTSIDE IN THE DARK THE RAIN</small> whipped against the windows of our tavern, making a sound like muffled drums. We were concentrating on our dinner, and everybody jumped when the door slammed open and banged against the wall, making the plates rattle in their racks. My brother Sam was standing there, wearing a uniform. Oh my, he looked proud.

"Sam," my mother said. We hadn't seen him since Christmas.

"Shut the door," Father said. "The rain is blowing in." That's the way Father was—do right first, and then be friendly.

But Sam was too excited to pay attention. "We've beaten the British in Massachusetts," he shouted.

"*Who* has beaten the British?" Father said.

Sam shut the door. "We have," he said, with his back to us as he slipped the latch in place. "The Minutemen. The damn Lobsterbacks marched out of Boston yesterday. They were looking for Mr. Adams and Mr. Hancock and they marched up to Lexington. Some of the Massachusetts Minutemen tried to stop them there in the square, but there were too many British, and they got through and went on up to Concord looking for ammunitions stores. But the Patriots got the stores hidden mostly and they didn't find much. And then when they turned around and went back, the Minutemen hid in the fields along the roads and massacred them all the way back to Boston."

Nobody said anything. They were silent and shocked. I couldn't take my eyes off him; he looked so brave. He was wearing a scarlet coat with silver buttons and a white vest and black leggings halfway up to his knees. Oh, I envied him. He knew everybody was staring, but he liked being the center of attention, and he pretended it was just an ordinary thing and he was used to it. "I'm starved," he said, and sat down at the table. "I started out from Yale at six o'clock this morning and didn't stop to eat all the way."

There were seven of us at the table in the taproom. Mother and Father and me were there. Then there was the minister, Mr. Beach, who lived in Newtown but spent Saturday night here in Redding so he could preach in our church early Sunday morning. Then there was a couple of farmers from Redding Center I didn't know, and, of course, Sam. But still they all sat silent. I guess they figured that it was up to Father to speak first, seeing as Sam was his son.

My mother got up, fetched a plate from the rack, and filled it with stew from the iron pot on the fire. Then she drew Sam a pot of beer from the tap and put it all down in front of him. He was hungry, and he bent over his plate and began shoving in the food as fast as he could.

"Don't eat like that," Father snapped.

Sam looked embarrassed and sat up straight.

"All right, now," Father said. "Tell us the news again in an orderly manner." Father had a temper and I could see he was trying hard not to lose it.

Sam dug his spoon into the stew and started to fill his mouth, but suddenly he realized that if he began talking with his mouth full, Father would yell at him again, so he put the spoonful of stew back on his plate. "Well it's hard to tell it orderly, Father. There were so many rumors around New Haven last night that—"

"I thought it might be like that," Father said.

"No, no, it's true about the fighting," Sam said. "Captain Arnold told us himself."

"Captain Arnold?"

"Captain Benedict Arnold. He's Captain of the Governor's Second Foot Guard." He looked down at his stew. "That's my company." He looked up and gave Father a quick sort of scared look.

"That explains the fancy dress, I imagine," Father said.

"Captain Arnold designed the uniform—"

"Never mind, tell the story."

"Well, the beginning was when the Lobsterbacks—"

"By that I suppose you mean the soldiers of your King," Father said. He was still holding onto his temper.

Sam blushed. "All right, the British troops. From the garrison in Boston. They marched up to Lexington looking for Mr. Adams and the rest, but they'd got away. Somebody signalled them from some church steeple in Boston, so when the Lobst—British got up to Lexington there wasn't anybody there, except the Minutemen. Then the shooting started—"

Mr. Beach put his hand up to stop Sam. "Who shot first, Sam?"

[4]

Sam looked confused. "Well, I guess the British. I mean that's what they said in New Haven."

"Who said?"

"Well, I'm not sure," Sam said. "I guess it's hard to tell in a battle. But anyway——"

"Sam," Father said. "Who do you think fired first?"

"I don't know, Father, I don't know. But anyway——"

"I should think it might matter to know, Sam," Father said.

"Why does it matter?" Sam was beginning to lose his temper the way he did. "What right have the Lobsterbacks to be here anyway?" I thought it was pretty funny that he kept calling the British Lobsterbacks, when he was dressed in red, too.

"All right, all right," Mr. Beach said. "Let's not argue the point. What happened then?"

"Yes, sir," Sam said. "So anyway, some men were killed, I don't know how many, and then the British went on up to someplace called Concord looking for the ammunition stores there, but they didn't find very much and turned around and started back to Boston. That was when the Minutemen really peppered them; they chased them all the way back home." Quickly Sam began to eat his stew before they had time to ask him more questions.

"Damn it, that's rebellion," one of the farmers said. "They'll have us in war yet."

Mr. Beach shook his head. "I think men of common sense will prevail. Nobody wants rebellion except fools and hotheads."

"That's not what they say in New Haven, sir," Sam said. "They say that the whole colony of Massachusetts is ready to fight and if Massachusetts fights, Connecticut will fight, too."

Finally my father lost his temper and slammed his hand down on the table, making the plates jump. "I will not have treason spoken in my house, Sam."

"Father, that isn't treas—"

Father raised his hand, and for a moment I thought he was going to reach across the table and hit Sam. But instead he slammed it down on the table again. "In my house *I* will decide what constitutes treason. What have they been teaching you at college?"

Mr. Beach liked peace. "I don't think the people of Redding are anxious to fight, Sam," he said.

Sam was nervous, but being Sam, he was bound to argue. "You get the wrong idea from Redding, sir. There's a lot more Tories in this part of Connecticut than in the rest of the colonies. In New Haven there aren't so many Loyalists and in some towns there aren't any at all."

"Oh Sam," Mr. Beach said, "I think you'll find that loyalty is a virtue everywhere. We've had these things before—that vicious nonsense of those madmen dressing up like Indians and throwing tea into Boston Harbor, as if wetting a few hundredweight of tea would stop the mightiest army on the face of the earth. These agitators can always manage to stir up the passions of the people for a week or so, but it never lasts. A month later everybody's forgotten it—except the wives and children of the men who've managed to get themselves killed."

"Sir, it's worth dying to be free."

That made Father shout. "Free? Free to do what, Sam? Free to mock your King? To shoot your neighbor? To make a mess of thousands of lives? Where have you been getting these ideas?"

"You don't understand, Father, you just don't understand. If they won't let us be free, we have to fight. Why should they get rich off our taxes back in England? They're 3000 miles away, how can they make laws for us? They have no idea of how things are here."

It made me nervous to listen to Sam argue with Father. I could see that Mr. Beach wanted to quiet him down, too, before he and Father got into a real fight the way they sometimes did. "God meant man to obey. He meant children to obey their fathers, he meant men to obey their kings. As a subject of the Lord Our God I don't question His ways. As a subject of His Majesty, George the Third, should you

[7]

question his ways? Answer me this, Sam—do you really think you know better than the King and those learned men in Parliament?"

"Some of those men in Parliament agree with me, sir."

"Not many, Sam."

"Edmund Burke."

Father lost his temper again. He banged his hand down on the table once more. "Sam. There'll be no more talk on this tonight."

He meant it, and Sam knew he meant it, too, so he shut up and the conversation turned to repairs Mr. Beach wanted to make to the church. I was glad, too. It scared me when Sam argued with the grownups like that. Of course Sam was that way, always shooting out whatever came into his mind and sometimes even getting hit by my father for it. Father hardly ever hit me, but he hit Sam dozens of times, mostly for arguing. Mother always said, "Sam isn't really rebellious, just too quick with his tongue. If he'd only learn to stop and think before he spoke." But Sam couldn't seem to learn that. My mother hated it when Father hit Sam for speaking out, but there wasn't anything she could do about it, and anyway, she believed that Father was right, children ought to keep a civil tongue in their heads. I guess he *was* right, children are supposed to keep quiet and not say anything, even when they know the grownups are wrong, but sometimes it's hard. Sometimes I have trouble keeping quiet myself, although not near as much trouble as Sam.

Of course Sam was almost a grownup himself. He was sixteen; he'd been away at college for almost a year, so you couldn't really call him a child anymore. I guess that was part of the trouble; he thought he was a grownup, and he didn't want anybody to tell him what to do. Except, I could tell that he was still afraid of Father.

But to be honest, I wasn't sure if Sam was right about the fighting anyway. It sounded right when he said it—that we should be free and not have to take orders from people who were so far away, and all that. But I figured there had to be more to it than Sam knew about. Father had never gone to college the way Sam had, but still I was pretty sure that he knew more than Sam. Father was a grownup and maybe Sam thought he was a grownup, too, but as far as I was concerned he was just my brother. He couldn't scare you the way Father could.

Besides, it made me glad to have him come home, and I didn't want him to get into a big fight with Father and spoil it. I just wanted him to shut up until dinner was over and we could go up to the loft where we slept, and I could lie in the dark snuggled up next to him to keep warm and let him tell me stories about

Yale and the pretty girls he knew in New Haven, and getting drunk with his friends and his triumphs in his debates. Sam was a triumphant sort of a person. He always had some victories to tell about whenever he came home from college. Mostly they were in debates where he scored a telling point over his enemy or whatever you call them. He would say, "And then I scored a telling point, Tim." He'd explain to me what the telling point was, which I never understood, and then he'd say, "Tim, it was a great triumph, afterwards everybody crowded around me saying, 'That was a telling point, Meeker, a telling point.'" Sam couldn't boast about his triumphs to Father or Mother or Mr. Beach or anybody like that, because boasting was pride and pride was a sin, but he could boast to me about them, because I didn't care whether it was pride or not, they were interesting. And I guess most of his boasts were true: he was always bringing home some book in Latin or Greek with an inscription saying he had won it for some telling point he had scored. Of course the inscriptions were usually in Greek which I couldn't read, but I believed him.

So anyway, I didn't want Sam to get into a fight with Father. It would spoil the fun, and besides if it were a bad enough fight, Sam might run away. He'd done that a few times after a fight with Father. Usually he just ran away to Tom Warrups' hut up behind

Colonel Read's house. Tom Warrups was the last Indian we had in Redding. He was the grandson of a famous chief named Chief Chicken which is a funny name for a chief. He didn't mind having people sleep in his hut. It made a convenient place for Sam to run away to, because it was close enough so that he could come home without any trouble after he'd stop running away.

But Sam stayed pretty quiet during supper. The grownups didn't pay any attention to him, but I kept looking at him to admire his uniform and I could see that he was thinking about something. It worried me that it was something else for him to get into a fight with Father about. But finally supper was over with and he'd stayed quiet, and I figured he was safe. The grownups got up. "Sam, are you going to help me with the milking?" I asked.

"I can't, my uniform will get dirty."

"Take it off, then."

I could see he didn't want to do that. "My other clothes are still at Yale."

"Borrow some from Father."

"All right, all right," he said. "Go on out to the barn. I'll come in a minute."

I knew he'd stall as long as he could, but I went out anyway so as not to get into a fight with him myself. The barn is out behind the house. Actually the house is partly a store and partly a tavern, too. The main room is the taproom, with a huge stone fireplace, and barrels full of beer and whiskey and cider. There's the big table in the middle with benches down the sides, and then at the end opposite the fireplace, more barrels and bins full of things we sell to the farmers around Redding Center, and Redding Ridge, which is our part of the town. We sell things like cloth and needles and thread, and nails, knives and spoons, salt and flour, pots and pans, and some tools, although mainly if anyone wants tools they have to go to Fairfield for them.

Behind the taproom is the kitchen. There's an even bigger fireplace there; in fact it takes up one whole wall, and of course cupboards for storing food, and hams hanging from the ceiling and salted beef and salted fish in barrels, and honey in jars and wheat in sacks. And out through the kitchen door there's the muddy barnyard and back of that the barn. We have a cow named Old Pru, and a horse named Grey, and some chickens, ducks and geese; and the old sow and six young pigs. Sam and I used to look after the animals, but after he went to college I had to do it all by myself. I hate doing it, it's just a lot of work.

I went out. The barnyard was muddy from the April rain. I jogged across it, trying to find the least muddy spots, and went into the barn. Old Pru mooed at me; she was tired of waiting to be milked. I got down the wooden bucket from its hook and started to milk her. It's a boring job, and your hands get tired. I kept hoping Sam would come out, so I could talk to him without the grownups around. But he didn't come, so I began to daydream about being older and going to Yale with Sam and scoring some telling points myself and Sam being proud of me—even though I know that daydreams are sloth and sloth is a sin. And I got pretty far along in the daydream before Sam came in. He still had his uniform on.

"Are you going to help me with the animals?" I asked.

"I wasn't going to, but Mother said that idle hands make the Devil's work."

"All right," I said, "you can pitch down some hay."

"I'll get my uniform dusty," he said. He picked up a straw and leaned against the wall picking his teeth.

"I thought you were going to change."

"I couldn't find anything else to wear," he said.

"What a lot of swill. You just want to show off how famous you are."

"Not at all, Tim, I'd have been pleased to help had I been able to find suitable clothes."

I pointed Old Pru's teat at him and gave him a squirt. Milk splashed on the knee of his trousers.

"Damn," he said, jumping back. "You little brat." He wiped off his trousers.

"Help, then," I said.

"All right. I'll collect the eggs. What on earth happened to this basket?"

I'd stepped on it once when I was mad. "It got broken," I said.

"I can see that," he said. "How did you manage to do that?"

"Old Pru stepped on it," I said. "Just put some hay in the bottom."

"God, can't you do anything right, Tim?"

"Don't curse," I said. "It's a sin."

He picked up the basket. "How am I supposed to collect eggs with a hole in the basket?"

"Stop complaining," I said. "I have to do this every night while you're down at Yale scoring telling points and getting drunk with those girls."

"You know I wouldn't do anything like that, Tim. Drunkenness is a sin."

I giggled. "So is—what's that word for girls? Lasviciousness."

"Lasciviousness, stupid, not lasviciousness. I have a new song about girls, but it's too *lasvicious* for you."

"Please sing it to me," I begged.

"No, you're too young."

"No I'm not. Besides, if you don't sing it to me, I'll tell Father how many times you got drunk."

"Ssshh, all right, I'll sing it later," he said. "This basket is hopeless. Isn't there another one someplace?"

"There's a new one hanging up over there, but we're not supposed to use it."

"Why not?" Sam said. "What can they do to me?"

I didn't like it when he talked like that. It bothered me. "Listen, Sam, why do you always have to get into a fight with Father?"

"Why does he always have to get into a fight with me?" Sam said. He had got some hay in the basket and was hunting eggs under the hen roost.

"That isn't fair. He pays for you to go to Yale and sends you money for books; you ought to be nicer to him. You knew he'd get into a rage when he saw you in that uniform."

Sam stood there staring at me with the broken egg basket in his arms, and I knew he was trying to decide whether or not to tell me something. I had enough sense to keep still. Sam pretty usually blurts things out if you pretend you're not interested and don't beg to him to tell. I went on milking Old Pru.

Finally he said, "Suppose I told you I had to wear the uniform for a reason."

That gave me a shiver. "I don't believe it," I said. I did believe it, but the best way to get him to tell was not to get all excited.

"It's true, Tim. I'm going to fight the Lobsterbacks."

That scared me, but it excited me, too. I wondered what it would be like to shoot somebody. Still I said, "I don't believe you, Sam."

"Oh you'll believe it soon enough. Tomorrow I'm walking up to Wethersfield to meet my company. Then we're going up to Massachusetts to fight the Lobsterbacks."

I believed him all right. "Won't you be scared?"

"Captain Arnold says it's all right to be scared; the true brave man is always scared. At least that's what the sergeant said he said."

"You seem to be pretty proud of Captain Arnold."

"Oh, he's a marvelous horseman, and brave, and doesn't take any nonsense from anybody. He'll lead us through the Lobsterbacks like a hot knife through butter." He started collecting eggs again.

"You're really going to Massachusetts?" I asked. It seemed like a long way to me. "To Boston?"

"I don't know exactly. I think we're supposed to go to Lexington," Sam said. An egg fell out through the bottom of the basket. "Damn it, Tim, why don't you fix this thing?"

"I did fix it, but it broke again." I didn't say it was a month ago and I was too lazy to fix it again. Laziness was sloth and sloth was a sin. "Tell me about the war," I said to change the subject.

"I told all I know at dinner."

"Why did you come home?" I asked.

He stopped hunting for eggs, and stared at me again. Finally he said, "I can't tell you."

"Why not?"

"You'll tell Father."

"No I won't, I swear I won't." I shut my mouth; with Sam it was the wrong thing to beg.

"Yes you will."

"All right, don't tell me then, I don't care. I don't believe any of it anyway," I said. I had Old Pru nearly empty and began stripping her teats to get the last drops of milk out, as if I'd forgotten all about what Sam was saying.

He didn't say anything for a minute. Then he said, "Will you really *swear* you won't tell?"

"I thought you said you weren't going to tell me."

"All right, I won't," he said.

"I swear," I said.

"On your honor?"

"Yes."

"This is serious, Tim."

"I swear on my honor."

He took a deep breath. "I came to get the Brown Bess."

That shocked me more than him saying he was going to fight. The Brown Bess was the type of gun most everybody around Connecticut had. It was brown, and got its name from Queen Elizabeth, whose nickname was Bess, because they first used that type of gun a lot during her time. The gun was about as long as I was tall, and had a bayonet around twenty inches long. Father kept the bayonet hanging over the mantelpiece. He used the Brown Bess for deer and sometimes when he went out with the other men to go after a wolf that was getting into the livestock. And he took it with him every fall when he went over to Verplancks Point to sell cattle and buy supplies for the store. He'd never met up with any trouble going over to Verplancks, but people he knew had sometimes been held up and robbed. So you can see that the gun was important to us. It was one thing for Sam to say he was going to fight the British; they were a long way from here. But to take Father's gun was pretty bad; Father was right here and he seemed a lot more real to me than the British did.

"Sam, you shouldn't do that," I said.

"I told you it was serious," Sam said.

Now I wished he hadn't told me. "You oughtened to do it, Sam. Father'll kill you."

"If I don't have the gun, some Lobsterback will kill me. Besides, it belongs to the family, doesn't it? I have as much right to it as anybody, don't I?"

I knew that was wrong and I shook my head. "It doesn't belong to the family; it belongs to Father."

Neither of us said anything for a minute. Then Sam said, "You swore, Timmy. You swore an oath."

I wished I hadn't. I was afraid to go back on my oath, but I was just as scared of Sam stealing the Brown

Bess, too. "Let's finish up with the stock and go to bed."

I figured if we went to bed he'd fall right asleep because he'd walked thirty miles up from New Haven that day. In the morning we'd all have to go to church —it was the law to go to church on Sunday—and it would be hard for him to steal the gun with people milling around and coming over to the tavern the way they did after church.

I finished milking Old Pru. Sam took the eggs up to the house and came back, and we fed the stock and watered them. We didn't say much. I knew that Sam was sorry he'd told me, and I was thinking of ways to stop him from doing it. Finally we were through. "Let's go to bed," I said.

"All right," he said. "Go on up, I'll be up in a minute, I want to talk to Father."

"Please come right up, though."

"Don't worry, Tim. Just go on up to bed."

I didn't want to leave him; but I knew there wasn't any use in arguing, so I said goodnight to Father and Mother, said some prayers, and went upstairs. There are four bedrooms on the second floor of our house, where lodgers stay when we have them. We get a lot of people traveling through between Stratford and Danbury, and Litchfield and Norwalk, or even going over to New York, and they need places along the way to sleep. Above the second floor is the loft where Sam and I sleep. There isn't much in it—just a couple of beds. There are no stairs up to the loft—just a ladder. I climbed up, not bothering to take a light. I knew where everything was. Besides, there are cracks in the floor which let little pieces of light through, so you can see a little if you have to. I undressed, got into bed, and pulled the blankets over me. I was always pretty tired by the time I went to bed, with all the chores I had around the tavern every day, but I wanted to stay awake to wait for Sam, so he could tell me some stories about telling points. To keep from falling asleep I lay on my back staring up at the black and watching the dots shift around in front of my eyes. But my eyes kept closing. So I began reciting all the books of the Bible from first to last, and I got to somewhere around Obadiah before I fell asleep.

When I woke up somebody was shouting. I sat up in bed. It was Father. I couldn't hear the words, but I could hear the sound—his heavy, hard voice going on and on. Then there was Sam's voice and he was shouting, too, and then Father again. I got out of bed, climbed quietly down the ladder, and crouched by the top of the stairs.

"You are not having the gun," Father shouted. "You are *not* going to Wethersfield and you are going to take off that uniform right now, if you have to go to church tomorrow naked."

"Father—"

"I will not have subversion, I will not have treason in my house. We are Englishmen, we are subjects of the King, this rebellion is the talk of madmen."

"Father I am not an Englishman, I am an American, and I am going to fight to keep my country free."

"Oh God, Sam fight? Is it worth war to save a few pence in taxes?"

"It's not the money, it's the principle."

"Principle, Sam? You may know principle, Sam, but I know war. Have you ever seen a dear friend lying in the grass with the top of his skull off and his brains sliding out of them like wet oats? Have you ever looked into the eyes of a man with his throat cut and the blood pouring out between his fingers, knowing that there was nothing he could do, in five minutes he would be dead, yet still trying to beg for grace and not being able because his windpipe was cut in two? Have you ever heard a man shriek when he felt a bayonet go through the middle of his back? I have, Sam, I have. I was at Louisbourg the year before you were born. Oh, it was a great victory. They celebrated it with bonfires all over the colonies. And I carried my best friend's body back to his mother—sewed up in a sack. Do you want to come home that way? Do you think I want to hear a wagon draw up one summer's morning and go out to find you stiff and bloody and your eyes staring blank at the sky? Sam, it isn't worth it. Now take off that uniform and go back to your studies."

"I won't, Father."

They were silent. It was terrible. My heart was pounding and I could hardly breathe.

"Sam, I'm ordering you."

"You can't order me anymore, Father. I'm a man."

"A man? You're a boy, Sam, a boy dressed up in a gaudy soldier's suit." Oh, he sounded bitter.

"Father—"

"Go, Sam. Go. Get out of my sight. I can't bear to look at you anymore in that vile costume. Get out. And don't come back until you come dressed as my son, not as a stranger."

"Father—"

"Go, Sam."

There were sounds. I could hear Father breathing as if he had climbed a mountain. Then the door slammed. I was afraid Father would come up so I slipped away from the top of the stairs and began to climb the ladder up to the loft. But then I heard some more sounds, some funny ones, sounds I'd never heard before. They puzzled me. I slipped back to the stairs and softly began to ease myself down them a step at a time. About five steps down I could see into the taproom. Father had his head down on the table, and he was crying. I'd never seen him cry before in my whole life; and I knew there were bad times coming.

My father's name was Eliphalet, but everybody called him Life. My mother's name was Susannah. Father was born in Redding where we have our
tavern, but Mother was born over in New York. He
had cousins over there where she used to live. Their
names were Platt, which used to be Mother's name.
I'd never met them, but when Father went over to

Verplancks Point every year to sell cattle and buy supplies he stayed with them and caught up on the news.

Redding wasn't much of a town compared with places like New Haven—although actually I'd never been to New Haven. About the only big place I'd ever been was Fairfield, down on Long Island Sound, where I used to go sometimes with Father and Sam to pick up sugar or rum that came up from the Barbados in big ships. There were thousands of people in Fairfield, at least it seemed like that, but there were only a few hundred in Redding.

Redding was divided into two parts—Redding Center and Redding Ridge, which was where we lived. Our tavern was at a corner where the Danbury–Fairfield Road met Cross Highway. Across the Danbury–Fairfield Road from us was the church and the graveyard. Next to the church, on the other side of Cross Highway was an empty field where the trainband practiced drilling. Next door to us was the Betts' house, and scattered around were a dozen more houses—the Sanford's house and the Rogers' house and Mr. Heron's house and some others. Our tavern was finished with shingles, but some of the richer people, like Mr. Heron, had white clapboard siding on their houses.

Our church in Redding Ridge was the Anglican Church. "Anglican" meant English Church; in England everybody had to belong to it, or at least they were supposed to. In Connecticut we had freedom of religion so you could belong to any church you wanted, unless you were a Papist. But there were hardly any of them in Connecticut. Over at Redding Center there was a Presbyterian Church; naturally, if you were a Presbyterian, you built your house over there and if you were an Anglican, you built here on the Ridge, although of course there were lots of farmers all around who didn't live near either church and just went to the one they wanted.

Because our church was the English Church, the people here on the Ridge seemed to be more on the Tory side and wanted to be loyal to the King. To tell the truth, I didn't exactly understand what the argument was all about. Ever since I could remember, all my life in fact, there had been these discussions and arguments and debates about whether we ought to obey His Majesty's government or whether we should rebel. What kept confusing me about it was that the argument didn't have two sides the way an argument should, but about six sides. Some people said that the King was the King and that was that, and we ought to do what he said. Other people said that men were supposed to be free to govern themselves and we should rebel and drive the Lobsterbacks out altogether. Some others said, well, they were born Englishmen and they wanted to die Englishmen, but that the Colonies ought to have more say in their own government, and that maybe we'd have to give the Lobsterbacks a taste of blood just to show the King that we meant business. Oh, people had all kinds of ideas—that we New Englanders ought to join together, or that all the Colonies ought to set up one big government or that—well I don't know, I can't even remember all the different sides there were to the argument. You can see how confusing it was when you realize that sometimes Sam's side was called Patriots and sometimes they were called Rebels. I guess I'd been reading newspaper stories about it and hearing people shout over the whole thing for so long that I didn't listen anymore—it just went in one ear and out the other.

But now it seemed like it wasn't going to be just arguments anymore. Around fifty of the Minutemen and lots of British troops had been killed on Friday at Lexington or Concord, or wherever it was, although nobody seemed to know how many for sure. And Sam was going to fight.

Sunday morning was bright and sunny and warm. The rain had stopped during the night. Although the road was full of mud, the fields were drying and the birds were singing. I couldn't enjoy it very much, though; the fight Sam had had with Father the night before still hung around me the way a bad dream does sometimes. Sam and Father had had fights before, and they always got over them in a day or two. But this one seemed worse than the others, and it worried me that maybe they wouldn't fix it up.

I didn't think Father would want to talk about it. Usually when something important happened he would just ignore it until he'd decided what to do. So I was surprised that he brought it up when we were getting ready to go to church.

"Tim, did Sam say anything to you about going to the war?"

I didn't want to lie to Father, but I didn't want to give Sam away, either. "Well, he said he was, but I thought he was probably just boasting."

"He wasn't boasting, Tim. He's going over to Wethersfield. The fools are planning to march up to Massachusetts to meddle in something that isn't their affair."

"Is he really going to fight, Father?"

"I hope not," he said. Then he frowned. "What do you think of all of this, Tim?"

"I don't know, Father," I said. "I can't figure out exactly what it's about."

"I suppose Sam's been preaching rebellion to you."

I tried to think of something that wouldn't get Sam in any more trouble. "He said we ought to be free."

"That's just college-boy wind," Father said. He sounded pretty scornful. "Who isn't free? Aren't we free? The whole argument is over a few taxes that hardly amount to anything for most people. What's the use of principles if you have to be dead to keep them? We're Englishmen, Timmy. Of course there are injustices, there are always injustices, that's the way of God's world. But you never get rid of injustices by fighting. Look at Europe, they've had one war after another for hundreds of years, and show me where anything ever got any better for them. Well, let's go to church. It's a time for prayer."

I decided to forget about the whole thing; it was too worrying. We went out across the muddy road to church, and I climbed up into the balcony where the children, Indians and black people sat. Redding Ridge being a small place I knew everybody there—all the kids, and Tom Warrups and Ned, the Starr's black man. I sat down next to Jerry Sanford. Jerry was a couple of years younger than me, but he was the person closest to my age around and we did a lot of things together. And the first thing he said was, "We heard Sam ran away to fight."

Nobody was going to let me forget about it, that was sure. Mr. Beach made it the subject of his sermon. He really got wound up on it, too. He said that our first duty was to God but that our Lord Jesus Christ had said, "Render therefore unto Caesar the things which are Caesar's" and that meant we were supposed to be loyal Englishmen. He said that hot-tempered young men who listened not to the voices of their elders would bring a wrathy God down on their own heads. He said that the Bible commanded youth to honor their fathers, which made me pretty nervous for Sam, because it was a sin to shout at your father the way he had done, and maybe God would punish him for it.

I didn't think that God would strike him down with a bolt of lightning or anything like that. I knew that God *could* shoot bolts of lightning if He wanted to, but I didn't believe that He ever did. What worried me was that maybe God would punish him by getting him bayonetted by a Lobsterback. I knew that God did things like that because I saw it happen once. A farmer from the Center came down here one Sunday very drunk and rode his horse through the burying ground, and when Mr. Beach told him to get out, he told Mr. Beach to go to hell and started to gallop his horse at Mr. Beach. But before the horse got more than two or three paces he tripped on a headstone and the farmer fell off and broke his neck and was dead a minute later. It's a true story; there were scores of witnesses.

So I knew that God could get Sam if He wanted to; and between worrying about that and being confused over which side was right I couldn't concentrate on church much. I just wanted to get out of there. But Mr. Beach always preached at least an hour and being fired up about the Lexington battle he went on longer. Fortunately, he always had to get back to Newtown to conduct service there in the afternoons, so finally he had to stop; and we finished up the service, and I breathed a sigh of relief and got up and started to file toward the stairs. I was nearly there when somebody touched me on the arm, and I turned around.

It was Tom Warrups. Tom didn't look much like an Indian. He wore the same kind of brown shirt and trousers any farmer around Redding wore, and he spoke pretty good English. "Hello, Tom," I said.

He didn't say anything, but he clutched me by the arm and sort of held me back, while the others filed past us down the balcony steps. Then he said in a low voice, "If I tell you where Sam is, you don't tell nobody?" He looked at me hard, and squeezed my arm—not enough to hurt, but enough so I knew he could hurt me if he wanted.

"Is he up at your place, Tom?"

"You don't tell nobody, Timmy. You get Tom in trouble."

"I won't tell, Tom." I wouldn't either—Tom scared me.

He let go of my arm, turned and went down the stairs. I came along behind him. My parents were standing out in front of the church, talking to people. It was always the same. Church was practically the only time we ever saw some of the farmers from farther out in the parish—places like Umpawaug. They wanted to keep up with the news, and Father always spent some time with them—it was good business, Father said, to be cordial with people. I knew they wanted me to stand around and be cordial too, so I did, but mostly Jerry Sanford and I threw little stones at each other, until Father caught us and made us stop. I was impatient to go see Sam, but of course I had to pretend I wasn't in any hurry to go anywhere, and the talk dragged on—all about the war and what might happen. Finally my parents got done talking, and we started to cross the street.

"Father," I said, "Jerry Sanford wants me to help him carry up a big log from the woodlot."

"That's breaking the Sabbath," he said.

"Well, it won't take very long."

He just shrugged. I guess he had too many other worries on his mind to get upset about that. So instead of going into the tavern I turned and went up the road to the Sanford's house. As soon as I got past it, so nobody could see me from the tavern, I climbed over the stone wall into Sanford's pasture and began running across the fields towards Colonel Read's house. It was a couple of miles there going around by the roads, but by cutting across the fields I could make it in fifteen minutes. Better yet it brought me in from the rise be-

hind the house where Tom Warrups' shack was. If anyone from the Read's house saw me go up to Warrups'
they'd want to know why. I jogged along quickly. I
was pretty nervous—about lying to Father and about
what Sam was doing—but it being such a beautiful day
helped me to feel better. The sun was warm on my
shoulders, birds twittered and there was that spring
smell of mud and grass in the air. I just jogged along
not thinking about anything very much; and fifteen
mniutes later I came upon Warrups' shack.

It was made in the Indian way of a circle of poles
stuck in the ground with their tops bent together and
tied. Covering the poles were hides and rags and in
some places patches of straw thatch. There was a thin
trail of smoke coming out of the top where the poles
met. The door was just a hole in the side covered with
a blanket flap, but the flap had been pulled aside to let
light in. I ducked down and looked through the hole.
Sam was sitting on the ground with Betsy Read, holding hands. They looked pretty serious.

"Hello Tim," Betsy said.

"Hello," I said, slipped inside and hunkered down
by the fire. The fireplace was just a circle of stones in
the middle of the floor. There was a bed made of a
couple of deer hides stretched across a frame, a few pots
and pans and not much else. "I can't stay very long, I
told Father I was helping Jerry Sanford move a log."

"Oh, Father," he said. He sounded bitter.

"I heard your fight," I said.

"I'm too old for him to tell me what to do anymore," Sam said.

"This morning he said you were full of college-boy wind," I said.

"That's because I wouldn't obey him." He picked up a stone and began jiggling it from hand to hand. "I guess he's still mad at me."

"He cried last night after you left, Sam, maybe he knows something about wars that you don't."

Nobody said anything for a minute. I picked up a stick and began to push it into the fire to see it burn. Then Betsy Read said, "Timmy are you on your father's side or Sam's?"

I wished she hadn't asked me that question. I didn't want to answer it; in fact, I didn't know how to answer it. "I don't understand what it's all about," I said.

"It's simple," Sam said. "Either we're going to be free or we're not."

Betsy touched his arm. "It isn't that simple, Sam. There's more to it."

"What side is your family on, Betsy?" I asked.

"Oh, we're all Patriots. After all, my grandfather is head of the militia."

Her grandfather was Colonel Read. Her father was Colonel Read's son, Zalmon Read. They lived not far

[33]

from Colonel Read. "Is your grandfather going to fight the Lobsterbacks?"

"I don't think so," Betsy said. "He's too old. He said he would probably resign his commission to some younger man. Anyway he doesn't think we ought to fight unless we really have to. He says there ought to be some way of working it out with the King and Parliament without having to fight."

"There isn't any way to work it out," Sam said. "The British government is determined to keep us their slaves. We're going to fight."

"A lot of people aren't going to fight," I said.

"Around here they aren't. This is Tory country. Father, Mr. Beach, the Lyons, the Couches—most of them in our church are Tories. And they think it's the same everywhere, but it isn't. Down in New Haven they're ready to fight, and Windham's already marched their militia to Boston." He was being scornful. Sam always got scornful when other people disagreed with him, because he always thought he was right, although to be honest, a lot of the time he was right, because of being so smart. But still it was hard for me to think that Father was wrong.

"Sam, Father says for most people it isn't being free, it's only a few pence in taxes."

"That's Father for you, it's the money that counts. There are principles involved, Tim. Either you live up to your principles or you don't and maybe you have to take a chance on getting killed."

"Who wants to get killed?"

"Nobody *wants* to get killed," Sam said. "But you should be willing to die for your principles."

"That's right," Betsy said.

"But Betsy, you don't have to take a chance on getting killed," I said.

"I'd fight if I could," she said.

I hated arguing about it. "Well maybe the King will change his mind and get the Lobsterbacks out."

Sam shook his head. "He won't. He thinks he's going to teach us a lesson. But we're going to teach him one. We already taught him one at Lexington."

"That's what I mean," I said. "Maybe he'll give up now."

Betsy shook her head. "He won't. Not according to my father."

Everybody was quiet for a minute. Then Sam said, "There's going to be war. Which side are you going to be on?"

I couldn't answer. Sam made it seem that he was right and Father was wrong; but I didn't see how I could go against Father. I didn't say anything.

"Tim, you could help us by keeping an ear out in the tavern. With all the Tories around Redding there'll be lots of talk about what the Lobsterbacks are up to. You could find out who the Tories are—who's on our side and things like that."

It made me nervous to think about it. "I won't hear anything like that."

"You could be a big help," Sam said. "You could be a hero."

I stood up. "I have to go. Father'll get suspicious."

Sam got up, too. "Well, think about it," he said.

Betsy stood. "Tim, I'll see you around the tavern, if you hear anything."

But I wasn't paying attention to what she said, because as she stood up the shadows shifted and the firelight fell on the wall of the hut. There was a blanket lying there as if somebody had just thrown it down. But it hadn't just been thrown down accidentally, because sticking out from one end of it was the stock of a gun.

"Sam," I shouted, "you stole Father's Brown Bess."

He jerked around to look at it. "Damn," he said, "I didn't want you to see that."

"Sam, you can't take that. It's not yours, it's Father's."

"Sshh, don't shout so loud. I have to have it, Tim; I need it to fight with."

"Sam, you can't take it, we need it at home. Father needs it."

"You don't expect me to fight without a gun, do

you?" He gave me a sharp look. "Are you going to tell Father I'm still here?"

"Timmy," Betsy said, "you don't want your brother to get killed, do you?"

I stood there confused and mixed up inside. I didn't say anything.

"Are you going to tell?" Sam said again.

"Sam, please don't take it." I knew I was about to cry. "Please, Sam."

"I have to have it, Tim."

"Timmy," Betsy said. "You don't want Sam to get killed, do you?"

"Please, Sam."

"Are you going to tell?" Sam said.

Then I couldn't hold back anymore and I began to cry. "No, I won't tell," I whispered. "Good-bye."

And I turned and ran out of the hut and out across the field. About halfway home I got ashamed of myself for crying and stopped; and by the time I reached the tavern I'd got my eyes back to normal and nobody noticed.

III

It's a funny thing. You'd think that if there was a war going on in your own country, it would change everything, it would make your life different. You'd think that there'd be men marching and drilling and people hurrying back and forth and lots of talk about the fighting. But it wasn't that way at all; it wasn't any different from usual, it was just normal.

Of course there were battles. There was a battle at Bunker Hill where the Patriots massacred the British troops before they were driven off, and the Rebels also took Fort Ticonderoga without much of a fight. But these battles all seemed far away—they were just things we read about in the *Connecticut Journal* and the other newspapers. Sometimes Father brought home *Rivington's Gazette* from Verplancks. It was a Tory paper and he wasn't supposed to have it; it was illegal, so he kept it hidden. It made me wonder how the war was going to make us freer if you couldn't read any paper you wanted any more. Oh, I don't mean that we ignored the war. There was always a lot of discussion about it around Redding, and sometimes people in the tavern would get into arguments over it when they'd drunk too much whiskey. Once Father actually threw a man out of the tavern. He was a stranger, and I guess he didn't realize that Redding was such a Tory town because he told somebody that the only good Lobsterback was a dead Lobsterback and that King George was a great hairy fool. My father said, "That's subversion and we don't permit subversion here."

The man smacked his beer mug down on the table. "I thought I was among free men, not slaveys."

He hardly got the words out before Father jumped over to the man, jerked him out of his chair and pushed him through the door into the mud of the street. The man lay there on his back cursing Father, but Father slammed the door and the man left. I guess he suddenly realized that he was in Tory country.

But leaving out things like that, the war didn't affect us much around Redding in that summer of 1775. Except for Sam. Sam was gone and nobody mentioned him—not Father, not Mother, not me. Father didn't mention him because he'd kicked him out, and Mother and I didn't mention him because of not wanting to get Father angry. For all we knew, Sam could be dead. But I didn't want to think about that, so I didn't.

So the summer went along and I lived my ordinary life, which was mostly chores all day long. Having a father who was a tavern-keeper was a lot better than being a farmer's son, like most boys. Running a farm is terrible hard work—plowing and hoeing and milking cows and such and being out in the fields all by yourself with nobody to talk to all day long. Being around a tavern is a lot more fun. There are people coming and going, and a lot of them have been to the big towns like Hartford or New Haven or even New York or Boston, and they have stories to tell. But still, it isn't as much fun as people like Jerry Sanford think. Mostly Jerry works on his uncle's farm, and he thinks I have it lucky. He doesn't realize that there's an awful lot of wood to cut to keep the fireplaces going for cooking and a lot of water to come up from the well and if there isn't anything else to do, there's scrubbing the floors and washing the windows and keeping everything clean generally. My mother's strong on cleanliness. "Food tastes better in a clean house," she always says. And of course there's the livestock I have to care for, too. Besides, the woodlot is two fields down the Fairfield Road from the tavern and we have to cart it up.

So even if it was better than farming, it wasn't all that much fun. Of course whenever I could I ducked out and did something with Jerry Sanford. If it was hot, we'd go for a swim in the mill stream, or climb the trees up in his woodlot. We played mumble-the-peg or spin tops or play duck on the rock, which I usually won because I could run faster. Sometimes, if it rained we'd go up to Tom Warrups and get him to tell us stories about the Indian wars and the brave things his grandfather, Chief Chicken, did. Or if nobody was watching me, I'd sneak up into the loft and look at the old almanacs Sam brought back from college sometimes. But mostly I worked.

I saw Betsy Read a lot. She came into the tavern pretty often to buy thread or cloth or something, and I noticed that when she did she'd linger around on some excuse and try to listen to what people were saying until my mother would say, "Betsy, I don't think your mother intended for you to spend the day idling," and she'd go. I didn't see what difference it made, anyway: I never heard anyone say anything important.

Then one day in September she came down with a jug to buy beer. She sat down at the table, and when my mother had her back turned filling the jug, Betsy gave me a wink and jerked her head toward the door. I wrinkled up my forehead at her to explain what she meant, but she just nodded at the door again. Then Mother brought the beer jug back and put it down on the table. "Off with you, Betsy," she said. "Idle hands make the Devil's work." Betsy got up, picked up the beer jug and walked to the door.

"I forgot to put away the pitchfork," I said.

My mother gave me a funny look. "When were you using the pitchfork?"

"Did I say pitchfork?" I said. "I meant the water bucket, from when I watered the chickens this morning." I went through the kitchen and outside and then ducked around the corner of the house. When Betsy came out of the front door I gave her a low whistle, and she slipped up to the side of the house beside me and gave me a serious look. She wasn't much taller than I, but she was fifteen and of course she was smarter than I was. "Tim, I have to talk to you about something serious."

It was a beautiful sunny day. The birds were twittering and the breeze was blowing and you could smell the hay in the field next to us waving in the heat. The wooden shingles of the tavern were warm. It was too nice a day to worry about things. I bent my head and touched my cheek to the warm shingles. "It's about Sam."

"Tim, if he came back to Redding, would you tell your father?"

"I wish Sam would give Father back the Brown Bess."

"Tim, stop worrying about that; Sam needs the gun."

"I wish he would, though."

"Please stop worrying about it. Just tell me what you would do if Sam came back for a visit."

"Why does Sam want to fight with Father?"

"Please, Tim," Betsey said. "I have to go, just answer my question."

I still hadn't made up my mind which side I was on in the war, and I didn't care whether Sam was a Patriot or a Tory or what. All I could think about was snuggling up to him and listening to him talk about scoring telling points. Knowing Sam I was pretty sure he was trying to score telling points from the other soldiers he was with. "I won't tell," I said.

"Promise?"

"I promise."

"You swear on the Bible, Tim?"

"I swear on the Bible," I said. "When is he coming?"

"I don't know exactly," she said. "Soon. He sent me a letter."

I was disappointed. "He didn't even say when he could come?"

"No. I have to go, Tim. Remember, you promised."

But he didn't come soon. At first I thought he would come in a few days, but he didn't. A week passed and another week and still he didn't come. When I saw Betsy at the tavern or in church I would look at her in hopes that she would give me a sign or whisper to me that Sam was coming soon, but she never did. I guess she was scared of having the subject come up in front of grownups, especially Father or the other Tories. Once I actually managed to speak to her when she came into the tavern while Mother was in the kitchen getting some bread for some travelers who were eating lunch.

"When's he coming, Betsy?" I whispered. "When?"

"Ssshh, Tim," she hissed. "Just shush about it."

So I shut up about it, but I couldn't stop thinking about it. I wanted to have Sam there and listen to him talk about the fighting and everything. I wanted to tell him about everything I'd done, too, all the things that would make him proud of me and respect me, like finally being able to throw a stone clear over the tavern, which we weren't supposed to do, and about being best in school in arithmetic. I never used to be very good at anything in school, but for some reason I suddenly got good at arithmetic.

So September passed and then October. The geese flew south in long, wavering V's. The leaves went red and orange and then brown and fell so that they crunched when Father and I walked around on them out in the woodlot, where we were getting up the winter's wood. The sky went that low, November grey; the puddles grew coats of ice overnight, and one morning when I woke up the fields were white with snow. That morning Betsy came down to the tavern with the beer mug. Mother was out with the chickens, but Father was in the taproom sharpening the two-man saw, because we were going out to the woodlot.

"Hello, Betsy," Father said. "How's your family?"

"In good health, sir," she said.

"I'm glad to hear it. What can I do for you? Beer, is it? Well help yourself, you know where it is."

"Thank you, sir," she said. She crossed over to the barrel. Father bent over the saw, the file making the metal sing as he worked it over the teeth. "Tim, are you going to school this term?" Betsy asked.

"Yes," I said. I looked at her. "We started last month." Then I noticed that she was nodding her head slowly up and down. Sam was back.

I WAS SO EXCITED I COULD HARDLY STAND IT. I FELT
all sparkly inside—sort of scared and happy both at the
same time. When lunchtime came I could hardly force
myself to eat, although of course I did, so nobody would
suspect anything. Being so excited worried me. A couple
of times I almost blurted something out. You know how
it is when you get really interested in something, you

forget what you're doing or even where you are. Well
I was thinking so hard about going up to Tom Warrups'
and finally seeing Sam after all this time that I kept
forgetting it was a secret. Once I started to say aloud,
"I wonder if Sam really shot anybody," and another
time I began to say, "Maybe I ought to bring him up
something to eat." But both times I caught myself in
time.

The big question was to find an excuse to get away.
On a school day it would have been different, I would
have just told the teacher I had to go home and help at
the tavern, and gone up to Warrups'. But I didn't want
to wait until Monday; probably Sam would be gone by
then anyway.

After lunch Father sent me out to the woodlot with
the axe. Although it had warmed up some, the day was
cloudy and the thin layer of snow was still on the ground.
From the woodlot the whole country looked white, as
if it had been painted to match the church and the houses
around it. I began cutting wood, wondering if I dared
to sneak away to Warrups'. I decided not to: after a
while Father would notice that there weren't any chopping sounds and come up to see what I was doing. I
needed another excuse; and as I chopped I tried to think
of one.

I was thinking like that when I first heard the horses.
I straightened up, letting the axe dangle from my hand,

and listened. There were a lot of them coming up the Fairfield Road from the south and they were coming pretty fast. I stared down the road toward the bend. They would have passed right by me. At first all I could hear was the heavy drum roll sound of hooves; then I began to hear voices of men shouting and the jingling of harness. Then suddenly they came pouring around the bend of the road into sight. It was a party of maybe twenty people, and even at a distance I could see that some of them had on blue uniforms which meant that they were Continentals—the Rebel troops. I stood back among the trees and watched them come galloping by. It was a pretty unusual thing to see a party of horse-men in Redding. They came on, and then they were swirling by, an officer wearing a sword in the lead, fol-lowed by the ordinary soldiers. Most of them had Brown Besses like ours slung over their backs. I guess they were mostly from the Fairfield trainband. The horse-men pounded on, churning the snow on the road into mud. I kept down in the shadow of the trees, but they didn't pay any attention to me anyway. In a moment they had swept passed. I darted through the trees to the road, and looked after them. They pulled up at the tav-ern. The officer and three of the men dismounted, and then the rest galloped off.

I was scared, but I was curious. I figured the officer had gone into the tavern to drink a mug of beer. I hadn't really seen many true soldiers, and I wondered what they were like. I wasn't sure if it was safe, though. What would they do if they knew that Father was against the war? Still I didn't want to be left out of the excitement. So I cut back through the woodlot and across the snowy fields so I could come up to the house from behind. I figured I would sneak in the kitchen door and listen to what was going on first. I was still carrying the axe. It was dangerous to run with an axe, because you might fall and cut yourself, but it made me feel safer to hold it in my hand. I went on running through the light snow, and then I came up behind the barn and eased myself around it into the barnyard. I could hear the horses stamping and jingling their harnesses in front of the tavern.

Somebody began to shout. The shouting was coming from inside the tavern. I darted across the barnyard and slipped into the kitchen. The door to the taproom was mostly closed, but there was a crack where it was hinged onto the wall. The shouting went on. I tiptoed to the door and put my eye to the crack.

Mother was standing up against the fireplace wall. There was a man in front of her, holding a rifle sideways to keep her from getting away. Two other soldiers had hold of Father from the back, twisting his arms behind him so that he couldn't move. The officer in charge stood in front of him with a sword. "We know you have a weapon, Meeker. Where is it?" he shouted. He jabbed the sword forward as if he was going to stick it into Father, and at the same time the men holding Father gave him a jerk. I began to shake and shiver, and I thought I would run someplace to get help, but then I realized there wasn't any help. Probably the Patriots were trying to get the guns away from all the Tories.

"I don't have it anymore," Father shouted. "My loyal son Samuel stole it to go play soldier boy."

The officer laughed. "Come now, I'm not going to believe that story. You're all Tories here. We want your gun." He jabbed the sword again at Father's stomach.

"Believe it or not as you like," Father said. "What do you intend to do, run me through with that sword and leave my wife and child to fend for themselves?"

"I will if you don't give up your weapon." He jabbed again with the sword. "We know you have one. We know where all the Tory weapons in Redding are. Not everybody is willing to play the dog to the King."

My father spit. "There are traitors everywhere," he shouted.

"Watch your tongue or I'll slice it out."

Oh, it scared me to hear Father yell at the Rebel officer. I wanted him just to be quiet and not make a fuss; to beg, even. It made me realize where Sam got

his rebelliousness from, though. Father didn't like anybody to tell him what to do anymore than Sam did.
"Oh, Father," I whispered to myself, "please don't
talk back."

And I guess Father realized that he ought to be
more quiet, because he got a grip on himself and said
calmly, "I'm telling you the truth, my son ran off to
join your army and took my gun. We have no weapons
here but butcher knives."

The officer looked at Father, considering. Finally he
said, "I don't believe you." He raised the sword. I
gasped and the officer whipped the flat side of the blade
across Father's face. My mother shrieked, Father cursed,
and a thin line of blood appeared on his cheek and up-
per lip. I knew what I had to do. I ducked out of the
kitchen, dashed across the barnyard and began to run
through the pastures toward Colonel Read's house.
There was one person who knew what had happened to
Father's Brown Bess, and he was up at Tom Warrups'.

Oh, I was scared. The war had finally come to Redding, and it was terrible. I guessed pretty easily what
was happening. Because Redding had such a reputation
for being a Tory town, the Rebels had decided to disarm it—at least disarm the Tories. Partly it was to get
guns for themselves—everybody knew that the Rebels
didn't have enough of anything, guns included. And
part of the idea was to make sure that Redding Tories

wouldn't be able to do to the Continentals what the
Minutemen had done to the British at Concord and
Lexington six months earlier. And I knew the Rebels
weren't just playing; they'd kill Father if they wanted
to.

So I ran uphill and down, clambering over the stone
and rail fences that divided the pastures. My lungs began to burn and even though it was cold, my face was
soaked with sweat. But I didn't dare stop to rest; all I
could see in front of me was that Rebel officer pushing a
sword through Father's stomach. So I ran on, my breath
roaring in my mouth and my legs getting so weak and
trembly that a few times I almost stumbled.

Then I saw Tom Warrups' shack and I stopped running. There was a tiny trickle of smoke drifting up
from the chimney, which I could hardly see against the
grey sky. I slipped quietly around to the door. The
blanket was hanging across it. I pushed it a little aside
and peered in. The fire in the circle of stones was practically out, but there was enough light so I could see
that there was nobody in the hut but Sam. He was lying
on Tom Warrups' frame bed on his stomach, with a
deerskin rug over him. I could hear him softly breathe
and see his back go up and down. I guessed he must
have walked a long way to get to Redding and was
tired. He was a pretty good sleeper, anyway; I'd slept
with him all my life and I knew that he was hard to
wake up, even if you punched him.

I crept into the hut, leaving the blanket hanging over
the door in case somebody should walk by, and knelt
down by the bed. I was sorry to wake him up, knowing
how tired he must be. I put my hand on the bed to
shake it; and suddenly I realized I was touching something funny. I felt along the edge of the bed. There
was something hard and long under the blanket. I put
my hand under the blanket to feel it better, but already
I knew it was the Brown Bess. I guess Sam had got into
the habit of sleeping with it so nobody would steal it.
He was lying with his arm across it, with the blanket
over top of both.

Carefully I slid my hand down the barrel until I got
to the stock, gripped it, and gave it a little pull. Sam
snorted in his sleep and shook his head as if he were
trying to shake a fly off his face. But he didn't wake up.
I gave the gun another little pull. This time he began
to talk loudly, but the words came out nonsense, and I
couldn't make them out.

I let go of the gun and took my hand out from underneath the blanket, trying to think what to do next.
Sam was pretty tired, and being a good sleeper, I figured I might be able to move his arm without waking
him up. When we used to sleep together plenty of
times he'd thrown his arm or his leg over me in his
sleep, and I'd have to grunt and heave to get myself
untangled from him, and he'd never wake up. I decided to take a chance. I flipped the blanket back a little

until his arm and the Brown Bess were uncovered. Then I quickly bent his arm away so it wasn't lying across the gun anymore. He snorted again, but he didn't wake up. I picked up the gun, ducked through the door of the shack just pushing the blanket away with my head. When I got outside I began running across the snow-covered pastures as fast as I could go, praying that I'd get back before anything happened. Ahead of me, as far as I could see was a trail of my own footprints in the snow, drawn like a line across the fields and fences that divided them up.

I was so worried and scared that I didn't even hear Sam coming until I was across Read's pasture and climbing over a stone wall at the other side. As I slid over the wall, I first heard the heavy thump-thump of running feet. I looked back. Sam was down at the bottom of the pasture about a hundred yards away, charging up at me as fast as he could come. He saw me look at him, but he didn't shout, for fear that somebody would hear him.

I leaped over the wall and began running on as fast as I could, but I knew it was hopeless. Sam was bigger and stronger and faster than me. I looked back again. Sam was coming up to the stone wall. He didn't bother to climb it, he just cleared it in one jump and came running on. I turned and swung down to the left in the direction of the road. I didn't think Sam would follow me there for fear of being seen. I tried to pray, but I couldn't think of any right words and all I could do was whisper over my gasping breath, "Oh please, God, oh please, God."

And then Sam was ten yards behind me. "Timmy," he said in a whispery shout. "For God's sake, Tim, give me that before you hurt yourself."

I swiveled around to face him. He lunged at me, grabbing for the muzzle of the gun. He got a couple of fingers on it, but I jerked it out of his grip. He cursed, and stuck his fingers in his mouth, and I could see he'd got a little gash from the bayonet clip when I jerked it out of his fingers. I leveled the Brown Bess at his stomach and I said, "Don't come any closer, Sam, or I'll shoot you."

I couldn't even hold the gun right. It was too long and too heavy for me to hold against my shoulder the way you're supposed to. I had to hold it against my hip with one hand on the trigger and the other wrapped around the barrel. I knew that if I fired it I'd be knocked flat, but I didn't care.

Sam stared at me. "Timmy."

"Don't move, Sam."

"It isn't loaded, Tim."

"You're a liar."

He started to step toward me. "Stand back, Sam, or I'll shoot you in the stomach." Suddenly I began to cry, not just little tears but big sobs all mixed up with trying to get my breath. I felt ashamed of crying in front of Sam, and embarrassed, but it was all so terrible I couldn't stop.

"Timmy, don't be crazy. It isn't loaded. Now give it to me before it gets damaged."

"Jesus, Sam, Jesus, they're down there and they're going to kill Father if he doesn't give them the Brown Bess."

"Who? Who's down there?"

"Some Continentals, with some others from Fairfield."

Then he lunged. I never knew whether I would have pulled the trigger because the next thing I was lying on the ground with Sam on top of me, and he'd got the gun. My fingers hurt, and when I looked at them I saw that they were bleeding, too, where they'd got ripped out of the trigger guard. Sam's face was dead white. "You would have shot me, you little pig, wouldn't you?" He got up off me, and I sat up. "Are you all right?" he said.

I jumped up. "I wouldn't tell you if I wasn't, you son of a bitch. By this time they've probably killed Father."

"Timmy, I can't go down there."

"Why not? They're supposed to be your friends."

"I can't, Timmy, I'm not supposed to be here."

[56]

"What do you mean you're not supposed to be here?"

"I'm supposed to be in Danbury buying cattle. They sent me down from Cambridge with Captain Champion, the commissary officer because I'm from around here."

"Did you run away?"

"I didn't desert, I just came home for a couple of days. Captain Champion had to go over to Waterbury for something so I decided to slip home for a day or so."

"To see Betsy Read."

"All right, so what?" Sam said.

"Won't you get in trouble?"

"They won't catch me," Sam said. "People are always sneaking off home for a few days; the officers don't know where half the men are a lot of the time. If they come around looking for you, one of your friends says you sprained your ankle and you're coming along behind."

"Sam, I'm scared about Father. Let's not stand here talking."

He looked sort of uneasy. "He's probably all right. They've been disarming Tories in lots of places. It's orders from the Connecticut General Assembly. You don't think they're going to let the Tories keep their guns, do you?"

"What'll they do to Father?"

"Oh, probably just push him around a little. They don't shoot people."

"I saw him, Sam, he was going to stick his sword into Father. You *have* to go down, Sam, you have to."

"I can't, Tim. They might hang me for a deserter if they found out."

"All right then, let me take the gun home and give it to them."

"I can't do that, Tim. If I go back to camp without my weapon, they'll surely hang me."

I thought about that. "Oh God, Sam, what did you have to fight for? Why didn't you stay in college?"

"I couldn't, Tim. How could I not go when all of my friends were going?"

I understood that, but I wasn't going to give in. "Your family ought to be more important than your friends."

He looked embarrassed, but he didn't say anything.

"I think you're a coward," I said. I didn't really think that—anybody who joined the army to fight couldn't be a coward, but I was still angry at him.

"No, I'm not," he said.

To tell the truth, it was me who was being the coward. Now that I'd got calmed down a little, I was afraid of what I might find when I went home. Suppose I walked in and found Father lying on the floor with a hole in his stomach bleeding to death, and maybe Mother dead, too. "All right, Sam, if you're not a coward, come home with me and see if everything is all right."

He thought about it. "I'll go as far as the barn with you." Swiftly he loaded up the Brown Bess, with powder from the horn slung around his neck and pouch of shot he had dangling from his belt, and rammed it home with a ramrod.

It impressed me, the casual easy way he did it. "Did you ever kill anybody, Sam?"

He looked embarrassed again. "We haven't done any fighting yet."

We set off across the snow fields, uphill and down, the way I'd come. Sam set a pretty good pace. He was hard and strong and used to it, from all the marching he'd done, and I had a hard time keeping up; but I was glad to go fast because I was so worried about Father. In fifteen minutes we came to our road, crossed it, and circled around back of the house. We ducked into the barn and stared at the tavern. There was smoke coming out of the chimney, but that was all—no sounds, no sign of men, no horses.

"Nothing happening," Sam said.

"Come on in with me and see," I said.

"It's risky, Tim."

"There's nobody around," I said.

He stared at me. We both knew it was his job to go in because he was the older brother. "All right," he said. "Let's go."

We darted across the barnyard and into the kitchen,

and all of a sudden there was Father standing there, the line of blood drying on his face. He and Sam stood five feet apart, staring at each other. Then Sam turned and ran. "Sam," Father shouted. "Come back, Sam."

But Sam raced across the barnyard and then began pounding over the snowy field toward the woodlot, the Brown Bess under his arm. Father and I ran out into the barnyard and watched him go. Father knew he couldn't catch Sam. We watched him until he got to the stone wall at the edge of our pasture. He jumped up on it and stood there looking back at us. Then suddenly he waved, jumped down from the wall, and disappeared into the woodlot.

U p to that time the war hadn't been very real.
I mean I knew it was going on because of stories in the
Connecticut Journal, and from tales we heard in the
tavern—stories travelers would tell us about somebody
being killed or suddenly coming across some fresh
bodies in a field. One man who stopped with us had
been at the Battle of Lexington and had been wounded

in the knee there. He walked with a limp, and he had the ball that wounded him on a string around his neck. And of course Sam wasn't the only one from Redding who'd joined the militia; there were others, and every once in a while you'd hear about this one or that one having been in a battle and maybe having been killed or wounded.

But none of them were people I really knew and so the war had always seemed to me like a story—something that happened in some faraway place or faraway time, and didn't have anything to do with me. But after the search for weapons, I had a different feeling about it: it was real and it could come home to me, too.

Luckily, the troops hadn't really hurt anybody: a few of the men who'd put up a fuss like Father had got punched around a little, and Father had that cut which left a very thin scar you could hardly see. But even if nobody had got hurt, the people in Redding were good and angry about losing so many of their guns. Guns were valuable. It wasn't so much a matter of hunting —there wasn't too much game around, although some farmers occasionally got a deer or a muskrat for the pot. Mostly people wanted guns to go after the wolves that sometimes came down into the pastures after lambs, and for general protection.

The worst part of it was that food was already beginning to get short. Army commissary officers, like the one

Sam was working for, were buying up a lot of the live-stock to feed the troops. Sometimes soldiers would just take a couple of cows out of somebody's fields without paying for them, too. Both sides did it—the Patriots and the Tories. They weren't supposed to, they were always supposed to pay, but a lot of time at the end of a day's march they'd find that there wasn't anything for them to eat, and they'd just go out into a field, butcher a couple of cows, cut them up and carry them off to camp on their shoulders. It was a terrible thing to lose your milking cows because it meant no more milk or butter or cheese. There wasn't anything anyone could do about it, though. Oh, whenever it happened the people would get up a petition and complain, but it never did much good because the soldiers were gone and the beef was eaten.

By January of 1776 food was getting to be a real problem for us, too. It wasn't so much that we were going hungry, but that the meat and flour and rum and beer and everything else we needed to run the tavern and the store kept going up and up in price all the time. This forced us to raise our prices; then prices would go up again, and we'd have to raise them some more.

But still, the worst part of the war was missing Sam. Of course he'd been gone at college before, so I'd got used to the idea of having to do his share of the work and all that. But when he was at Yale I didn't have to worry about him all the time—worry that he'd be shot or get sick and die or something else. Although to tell the truth, I envied him, too. I could picture him in my mind standing on top of the stone wall by the woodlot, the Brown Bess cradled under his arm, waving at us.

He seemed so brave and grown-up, and I wished that I could be brave and grown-up like him, too. I didn't like the idea of being shot at or wounded or killed very much, but it seemed to me that it must feel wonderful to be able to load up a gun in the casual way he did it. I knew that to a younger brother everything your older brother does seems wonderful. I remember being little and watching Sam milk Old Pru and admiring him and thinking how clever he was. And then it got to be my turn to learn how to milk Old Pru, and I found out that there wasn't any glory to it; it was just hard work and made your hands ache. So I guess that being a soldier probably didn't have much glory to it, either, that it was mostly just a lot of hard work. But still, I envied Sam, and I wished I were old enough to do something glorious, too.

So time passed and the war went on. Sometimes we'd read about Patriot victories and other times about Tory victories. It all seemed confused. It was hard to tell who was really winning—partly because sometimes both sides claimed to have won the same battle. Father said, "The Rebels are damn fools, how can they expect to

beat the whole British army? They can win these skir-
mishes in the woods, but as soon as the British catch
them in pitched battle they'll be done for, and no good
can come out of it but a lot of men dead." Sometimes
Patriot militiamen would come through Redding, and
usually the officers would come into the tavern for a
mug of beer, but they never bothered anybody, they
just went away again. I'd stand at the door and watch
them go; and I wondered, if I went for a soldier, which
army would I join? The British had the best uniforms
and the shiny new guns, but there was something exciting about the Patriots—being underdogs and fighting
off the mighty British army.

So it became spring; and one April morning in 1776
Mr. Heron came into the tavern with Tom Warrups.
There was a soft rain falling and a fire burning in the
fireplace. Father was rushing a chair seat, and I was
helping him. It all seemed warm and cozy.

Father stopped his work. "Good morning, Mr.
Heron," he said. Father was always polite to Mr.
Heron. He'd been to Trinity College in Dublin, and he
was a surveyor. He'd been elected to the General Assembly in Hartford, but he'd been pushed out of it by
the Patriots for being a Tory. He was rich, too, although nobody knew where he got his money from.
He owned a black man and he had other servants besides.

"Good morning, Life," he said to Father. Then he noticed me. "Good morning, Tim."

"Good morning, sir," I said.

"Life, you've got a smart boy there. Smart as Sam if he wanted to be. I hope he's going on with school."

My father shrugged. "I'd like him to, but I can't spare him from here every day."

Mr. Heron may have wanted me to go on with my schooling, but I wasn't so sure of it myself. I figured I was as smart as Sam, but I didn't have as much interest in school as he had. I liked ciphering all right, but I didn't care much for spelling and studying the Bible and memorizing psalms.

"Oh Sam's smarter than I am, sir," I said, just to be modest.

"I like to see him in school when I can," Father said, "but I need him here a good deal. I can't run the tavern without him."

"Still, it's a shame to waste talent. I could make a surveyor out of him if he'd apply himself. Perhaps I might take him on as an apprentice in a year or two, once he's learned to cipher."

Being a surveyor was a good thing. You could make a lot of money. Father said that surveyors always knew about the good deals on land and could get rich speculating. So that part of it sounded good; but I wasn't so sure about all that studying. "I don't know if I'm smart enough," I said, mostly to be modest again.

"Certainly you are, Tim." He sat down at the long table. "Tim, how about getting me a pint of beer? And one for Tom, too."

Tom Warrups did spare work for Mr. Heron; sometimes he ran messages for him, too. He didn't sit because he was only an Indian, but stood leaning against the wall. I got mugs down from the shelf and filled them, and served them around, including one for Father. He sat down at the table, too, and I went back to rushing the chair.

"What do you hear from Sam?" Mr. Heron said.

"Nothing," Father said. I knew he didn't want to talk about Sam, but he couldn't be rude to Mr. Heron.

"He never writes?"

"No."

They weren't paying any attention to me. I took a quick glance at Tom Warrups. He was standing there holding his mug of beer, his face blank. I couldn't figure out which side he was on. He lived on Mr. Read's land, and Mr. Read was a Patriot. But he ran messages for Mr. Heron, and Mr. Heron was a Tory.

"It's a shame about Sam," Mr. Heron said.

My father shrugged, but didn't say anything.

Mr. Heron must have known that Father didn't want to talk about Sam, but he said, "Perhaps there'd be a way of finding out where he is."

"If he wants to see us he knows where we live."

Mr. Heron nodded. "Actually I didn't come to talk

about Sam. I want to talk about Tim. I have a little job I thought Tim might do for me. I need a boy to walk down to Fairfield for me."

I watched Father's face. His eyes got narrow and he stared straight ahead. "Why a boy, Mr. Heron? What's wrong with Tom?"

Heron shrugged. "Pretty hard for a strange Indian to walk down there without getting stopped every five miles. Nobody's going to bother a boy."

It was a scary idea, but exciting. It would be a real adventure. But of course I knew that I wasn't supposed to have any opinion in the matter so I kept my mouth shut.

"What's he going to be carrying?" Father said.

"Oh just some business letters," Mr. Heron said casually. "Nothing important."

Father said nothing, but stared down into his beer. Mr. Heron took a drink. Then he said, "There's no danger, Life, nobody's going to bother a boy."

"Business letters," Father said.

"Yes. Business letters."

I couldn't keep my mouth shut any longer. "I can do it, Father. I can walk down there tomorrow morning and be back by suppertime."

"Be quiet, Tim."

"I'd pay him a shilling."

My father stared into his beer again and then slowly he began to shake his head. "No, Mr. Heron," he said.

"No. I've got one mixed up in this bloody war already. I'm not going to let the other one go."

Mr. Heron paused before he spoke. "I said they were business letters, Life. Business letters."

Father stared at him. "No, Mr. Heron. No."

When Father said no he meant no. It disappointed me. It would have been a good adventure walking down to Fairfield on my own. It was on Long Island Sound. I'd only been there two or three times in my life, when I'd gone down with Father and Sam to buy rum. Carrying letters down to Fairfield would give me something to boast about to Sam. But Father had said no. That was that and Mr. Heron knew it.

Mr. Heron finished his beer, and stood up. "I had more faith in you than that, Life," he said. "I thought I could count on you. We're all making sacrifices these days."

My father was standing, too. "I've made a sacrifice, Mr. Heron, I've lost a son. You know I have no love for the Rebels, but this is one war I'm not going to fight."

Mr. Heron nodded, and he and Tom Warrups left. I picked up the beer mugs to clean them. "I wish you'd have let me go, Father. Nothing would have happened to me."

Father put his hand on my shoulder. "Those weren't business letters, Tim."

"What?" I was surprised.

"I don't know what Heron's game is. He talks like a Tory all right, but it doesn't all quite make sense. Best thing is not to get involved with him. You can be sure any letters he's sending around aren't just about ordinary business. Now let's forget that he ever came in here."

He stared into my eyes and I stared back. "Yes, Father," I said.

But I couldn't forget about it. Mr. Heron had wanted me to carry some sort of war messages or spy reports or something, and that night as I lay in bed in the loft, I thought about it. Oh, it would scare me all right, walking down to Fairfield with spy messages, but I wanted to do it, because it would give me something to boast about to Sam. He'd been having all the adventures, he was going to come home with terrific stories about being in the army and fighting and all that, and I wanted to have something to tell, too. Why should he have all the glory? Why shouldn't I have some, too? I wanted him to respect me and be proud of me and not think of me as just his little brother anymore. I couldn't score telling points in debates the way he did, but I could be just as brave as he was and do daring things, too.

It made me angry with Father for not letting me go. It wasn't right—not with what Sam was doing. Of course Father hadn't let Sam go; Sam had run away.

But still it made me angry and thinking about it, I slammed the bed with my fist. If only I could find a way to sneak off for a day.

I thought about it some more the next morning when I was milking Old Pru and the more I thought about it the angier I got. By the time I had got Pru milked and driven out to the pasture, and fed the chickens and collected the eggs, and hung the milk down the well to keep it cool, I was plain boiling. It wasn't fair, that was all. And when I got back to the house I was angry enough to stand up to Father.

He was sitting at the taproom table drinking tea. I faced him and stood up as straight as I could. "Father, why can't I carry messages for Mr. Heron? You're on the Tory side, too."

He glanced at me and then blew on his tea to cool it. "Because I said so."

"That's no reason," I said.

He stared at me. "If you don't stop arguing with me, I'll thrash you, Timmy."

"I don't care," I said. "If we're supposed to be Loyalists, we should help—"

He slammed his fist down on the table and then jerked his thumb toward his chest. "I'll manage the politics in this family," he said.

"Father—"

"Timothy, goddamn it I'm going to—" And then he

[71]

stopped, and I knew why. He'd shouted at Sam and Sam had run away. He was scared that if he shouted at me I'd run away, too. "Tim, please," he said calmly as he could. "It's dangerous. You think that because you're only a child they won't hurt you, but they will. They've been killing children in this war. They don't care. They'll throw you in a prison ship and let you rot. You know what happens to people on those prison ships? They don't last very long. Cholera gets them or consumption or something else, and they die. Tim, it isn't worth it."

I knew he was right, that it wasn't worth taking the chance. I wanted to do it anyway. But there wasn't any use in arguing about it with Father.

Two weeks later I figured out how to do it. I was out on the road in front of the tavern trying to clean the mud and dirt off the boards we laid down there in the spring, when Jerry Sanford came up the road.

"Where are you going?" I said.

"The shad are running," he said. He held out a coil of fishing line with hooks and weights attached. "Father said I could try my hand at it."

"You're lucky. Look what I have to do."

"Ask your father if you can go."

"He won't let me. There's too much to do around the tavern."

"Ask him."

So I went inside to where he was holystoning the taproom table. "Father, Jerry Sanford is going after shad. Can I go?"

"You've got a lot of things to do here."

"If we caught a lot we could salt them down."

He thought about it. "All right, go. It would be a nice change to have some fish chowder."

So we went back to Jerry's house and got another line and some hooks, and then walked down to the millstream, which was really the Aspetuck River. There was a dam there for the mill, and below the dam a couple of hundred yards was a large pool. In the spring the shad ran upriver to breed, but they couldn't get past the milldam, and the pool was just swarming with them. We caught dozens. We had a terrific time. Father was pleased. He really enjoyed fish chowder. But best of all, I had my excuse to get away.

M<small>Y</small> <small>BIGGEST PROBLEM WAS GETTING TO SEE MR.</small>
Heron. If Father saw me talking to him, he'd be suspicious; and if he found out that it was me who started
the conversation, he'd know right away what it was all
about. But luckily two days later Mr. Heron came into
the tavern to buy a small keg of rum. My father wasn't
around, and Mother said, "Tim will bring it right
over, Mr. Heron."

So I slung the keg of rum over my shoulder and followed Mr. Heron up the road to his house, which was only a couple of hundred yards away from the tavern. We went around to the back, and I carried the keg into the kitchen and set it up on the rack. He reached into his pocket and handed me a penny.

"Thank you, sir," I said.

"Have you thought anymore about studying surveying with me someday?"

"Well I haven't, sir. But I was thinking though that I might like to earn some money at that job you mentioned before."

"Aha," he said. "Your father changed his mind, did he?"

"Yes, sir," I said. "He said it would be all right so long as he didn't know anything about it. If I just went and didn't tell him anything, he said he wouldn't object."

Mr. Heron put his hand on my arm and gave me a little squeeze. "That's a lie, isn't it, Timothy?"

I got hot and blushed. "I guess so, sir."

He let go of my arm. "Your father doesn't change his mind very often nor very easily."

I felt stupid and looked down at the ground. "Yes, sir," I said. "I'd still like to go, though. Aren't we supposed to be loyal to the King?"

He stroked his chin. "Not everybody thinks so."

"I do, though." I didn't—I mean I didn't have any

opinion either way—but I thought it would help if he believed that I was a strong Loyalist.

He smiled a kind of funny smile. "You've got your brother's spirit, haven't you?"

Being compared with Sam made me feel good. "I'm as brave as he is," I said.

"I believe it," he said. "Suppose I did let you run some errands for me. What would you tell your father?"

"I'd tell him I was shad fishing."

"And come home with no fish?"

"I'd tell him they weren't running or something. You can't always expect to catch something."

He rubbed his forehead, thinking. "All right. If you come up early tomorrow morning, I'll have something for you to do to earn a shilling or so."

So that night I asked Father if I could go fishing again. And he said yes. I felt sort of bad about it; it was lying, and lying was a sin, and so was going against your father. And even if it hadn't been a sin I would have felt badly about it, because Father trusted me and I was being dishonorable. But I wanted some glory too much to be honorable, so Wednesday morning I got up way before the sun, when it was just beginning to get light, took my fishing line and hooks to make my excuse hold up, and walked down to Mr. Heron's house.

I was lucky. It was a good day. That time of year

it could easily have been pouring rain, and cold. But as the sun came up there were only streaks of clouds in the sky. The birds were singing and the wild flowers along the roadside were bright and gay. I felt excited in a good way, and as I walked along to Mr. Heron's I began to whistle "Yankee Doodle" before I remembered that I ought to keep quiet so people wouldn't notice where I was going.

When I got to Mr. Heron's house I went around back to the kitchen door, and started to knock, but I had hardly got my fist up when the door jerked open, and Mr. Heron grabbed me by the arm and pulled me in. We walked down a hall and into his study. It seemed awfully rich to me. There was a little stove there with a few coals glowing and a desk piled high with papers and a carpet on the floor, and some chests of drawers. He sat down at the desk, wrote something out on a piece of paper, and sealed it up. "Timothy, you'll have to move quickly. This message has to go to Fairfield. It will take you at least five hours to walk down there and five to walk back, and you'll have to be home before dark in order not to raise suspicions. Have you ever been to Fairfield?"

"A couple of times," I said. "With Father and Sam to get rum."

"Then you know where the dock is. Now listen carefully. Just before you get to the dock there's a road off to the left. Down the road about a mile there's a house with white siding and green trim. Knock there. Ask for Mr. Burr. And give him this letter. He'll give you a shilling. Right? Now repeat it back."

I did so; then I tucked the letter down inside my shirt and left, slipping out the back way and through his pasture before I cut back onto the road. The sun was now up and was rising over the meadowland to the east. I judged it to be about seven o'clock. The sun wouldn't go down again until around seven at night, which gave me twelve hours—plenty of time if I walked along swiftly. In fact, if everything went well, I could easily be back by the middle of the afternoon, which might even give me time to catch a few shad to show Father. I hid the fishing tackle behind a stone wall just in case.

I moved at a brisk pace. Despite the sun, the air was morning cool and fresh. It was nice weather for walking and I felt excited, not scared. I was worried about dropping the letter, though, and I kept touching it to make sure that it hadn't fallen out of my shirt. After a while I came to the place where the road from the Center runs into the Fairfield Road. I stopped for a minute to rest and to see if I couldn't find a better way to stow the letter so it would be safe. I was trying to find a way to hitch it under my belt when I heard somebody shout. I looked up. Betsy Read was coming down the road from the Center.

"Hello, Tim," she said.

"Hello."

She came up to me. "What're you doing here? What's that?"

Hastily I shoved the letter back into my shirt.

"Nothing," I said.

"Well it isn't nothing," she said. "It's a letter." She smiled. "You've got a girlfriend."

"No," I said. "I have to go. I'm kind of in a hurry."

"I'll walk with you," she said. "Where are you going?"

It made me nervous having her walk along with me. She wasn't suspicious of anything, and I didn't think she would go down to the tavern and tell Father she'd seen me; but if she should happen accidentally to bump into him, she might say something. "I'm going fishing," I said.

"Fishing? On the Fairfield Road?"

"There are shad in the millstream."

"Well you're going in the wrong direction," she said.

"Oh. Well I know that, I was up there already, but there weren't any shad so I'm going someplace else now." I was blushing from telling so many lies. Lying is a sin.

"Don't you want to know where I'm going?" she said.

"Sure," I said.

"I'm going down to Horseneck. Guess what doing."

It was better to have her talk than me, because it saved me lying.

"I don't know. Shopping for cloth?"

"Guess again."

Horseneck was down on Long Island Sound, too, but much further south than Fairfield. I couldn't figure out what she might be doing there. "Visiting your cousins?"

"I don't have any cousins down there."

"What then?"

"Seeing Sam," she said.

I stopped dead in the road. "Sam? Is he in Horseneck?"

"I shouldn't tell you that. You're a Tory. Anyway he's not there anymore, they've gone someplace else."

We weren't walkng along anymore, but facing each other. I was all excited. "How do you know Sam's there?"

"Mr. Heron told me."

"Mr. Heron? How does he know, he's a Tory?"

She frowned. "Well I know that, but he said that Sam was there with a commissary officer, scouting for beef."

It didn't make any sense. Mr. Heron was supposed to be a Tory; he wasn't supposed to know where American commissary officers were. Suddenly I realized I I was wasting time. "Where is he now?"

"I won't tell you. You're a Tory."

"That's not fair, Betsy. He's my brother."

"God, Tim, you tried to shoot him."

I blushed. "Is Sam all right?"

"Yes, he was in battle—I guess I better not tell you about it."

"You can tell me if it already happened, can't you?"

"I better not," she said.

"Listen," I said, "I better get going."

We started walking. "Where are you off to in such a rush?" she said.

"If you won't tell me anything, I won't tell you, either." I thought that was a pretty smart answer; it was like one of Sam's telling points.

"All right, sulk," she said. "Besides, I know you're carrying a love letter for somebody."

"You've just got love on your mind because of Sam," I said. Something was puzzling me. "Betsy, how come Mr. Heron didn't tell me about Sam this morning?"

"Because you're a Tory."

"But so is he," I said.

She stopped. "What were you seeing Mr. Heron about this morning?"

I realized I'd made a bad mistake. "Oh I just happened to go by his house this morning and he was there."

"There? Where?"

"He was standing in the yard."

"Doing what?" she asked.

"How do I know what he was doing?"

"He wouldn't have been standing . . . the letter. Tim, you're lying. The letter. He gave you the letter to carry. Tim, where are you going with that letter?"

She was pretty excited and kind of bouncing around in front of me. "I have to go, Betsy."

She jumped in my way. "Oh no you don't, not until you tell me about the letter."

She was bigger than me, but not by much, and I figured that since I was a boy I could break away from her and run if she tried to stop me. "That's a private letter," I said. "I can't tell you about it."

"Oh no, Tim," she shouted. "Give me that letter."

"No," I said. I tried to duck past her, but she jumped in front of me again.

"Tim," she screamed. "You know what's in that letter? A spy report on Sam."

That shocked me. "It can't be. Why would Mr. Heron make a spy report on Sam?"

"Not on just Sam. Can't you see? He found out about Sam and the commissary officer buying beef, and now he's sending news to the Lobsterbacks so they'll know where to find them and kill them and steal the cows. Give me that letter."

She snatched at my shirt, but I ducked back. "Don't, Betsy. It's Mr. Heron's."

"Tim, you're going to get Sam killed. They'll set up an ambush for them and kill them all."

"No, no," I said.

"It's true, Tim, figure it out. You can't deliver that letter."

"I have to," I said.

She stood in front of me, kind of begging. "Tim, let's open it and see. If there's nothing important in it, then you can deliver it."

"I can't break the seal, Betsy. It's Mr. Heron's letter. I could be put in jail for that."

"Tim, it's your brother they're going to kill. Just throw the letter away and say you lost it."

I didn't know what to do. I felt awful—sick and scared. I didn't say anything.

"Tim, give me that letter."

"Betsy—"

Then she jumped me. She caught me completely by surprise. She just leaped onto me and I fell down backwards and she was lying on top of me, trying to wrestle her hands down inside of my shirt. "Goddamn you, Betsy," I shouted. I grabbed her by her hair and tried to pull her head back, but she jerked it away from me. I began kicking around with my feet trying to catch her someplace where it would hurt, but she kept wriggling

[83]

from side to side on top of me and I couldn't get in a good kick. I hit her on the back but in that position I couldn't get much force. "Get off me, Betsy."

"Not until I get that letter," she said. She jerked at my shirt, trying to pull it up. I grabbed at her hands and twisted my body underneath her to turn over so I would be on top, but she pushed her whole weight down on me, grunting. So I slammed her as hard as I could on the side of her head.

"You little bastard," she shouted. She let go of my shirt with one hand and slapped me as hard as she could across my face. My nose went numb and my eyes stung and tears began to come.

"Damn you," I shouted. I let go of her hand where she was clutching my shirt and grabbed her by the shoulders, trying to push her off me. She jerked my shirt up, grabbed the letter and jumped to her feet. Without rising I kicked out with my feet at her ankles. I got in a good one; she stumbled, but she didn't fall. By the time I got up she was running down the Fairfield Road as hard as she could, opening the letter as she went. I started to run after her, and then she flung the letter over her shoulder onto the road and disappeared out of sight around the next bend. I ran up to the letter and picked it up. It was rumpled and dirty. All it said was, "If this message is received, we will know that the messenger is reliable."

VII

THE SUMMER OF 1776 CAME AND WENT. I TRIED TO keep away from Mr. Heron. If I saw him coming into the tavern, I'd go out to clean the barn or down to the woodlot to do some chopping. But a few times he took me by surprise before I could get away. He never said anything about the letter at all. He'd just say, "Hello, Timothy," or "It's a fine day, isn't it, Timothy?" and

I'd say, "Yes, sir," or something like that and get away as soon as I could. I couldn't figure out what he thought about the whole thing, and finally I just forgot about it.

The war went on. It didn't seem to have much to do with us most of the time, aside from Sam being gone. Of course food was short, and other things, too. The men who still had their guns had trouble getting powder and shot. Cloth was getting scarce, and leather, because the Continental troops needed them for clothing and shoes. But nobody was really desperate.

Sometimes we'd be reminded of the war when militiamen marched through. Or we might see a soldier who had been wounded or whose enlistment was up walking back to his home. But mostly the war stayed away from us.

Twice we got letters from Sam. Or rather, Mother did. One came in August of that year and another one in September. The first one told about the fighting in New York. The Rebel troops had been beaten there, and the British had taken over the city, but the way Sam wrote about it, he made it seem like a glorious victory for the Rebels. He said that his regiment had made a magnificent retreat, and the British were lucky they'd got out of it alive, but it sounded the other way around to me. The second letter didn't tell so much, except that they were encamped someplace in New

Jersey and probably would stay there for the winter. He was living a hard life. A lot of times they were on very short rations, eating just hardtack and water day after day. They didn't have proper clothing, either. Some of the men had no shoes and went barefoot: in cold weather they wrapped cloth around their feet to keep from freezing. I guess there wasn't much glory in it a lot of the time, but Sam said that their spirits were high.

Mother and Father had a fight over the letters. When the first one came Mother decided to answer it. Father said no, she shouldn't encourage Sam in his recalcitrance. Mother argued with him, but he wouldn't give in: let Sam feel our disapproval until he comes to his senses. But then when the second letter came she said she was going to write an answer regardless. They had an argument about it when I was supposed to be asleep. I kept hoping Mother would win. It made me sad to think of Sam writing letters and nobody writing back, although I guess Betsey Read would write back. But Father didn't feel that way. "The boy has to learn a lesson, he's far too headstrong."

"He isn't a boy anymore," Mother said.

"He's sixteen years old, that's a boy, Susannah."

"He's seventeen, Life. How old were you when you left home?"

"That was different," he growled. "There were

eight of us, remember, too many mouths to feed as it was."

"Still, you went off at sixteen, Life."

"Sam's too headstrong."

"And you're not?"

"I'm his father, I don't have to be questioned on my behavior."

Mother laughed. "You hate having anyone tell you what to do, yet you expect Sam to let you order him around. I'm going to write to him, Life. He must surely be worried that we're all right."

"I don't want you to do it, Susannah."

"I know you don't, Life. But I'm going to do it anyway."

I heard Father make a grunting sound, and then the door banged, and he stomped out to the barn. In the dark I clapped my hands. I was glad that Sam was going to get a letter.

But by that fall of 1776 I didn't have much time for pondering over Sam or Mr. Heron. Father was planning his usual trip to Verplancks Point, and this year for the first time I was going with him. It was pretty nearly forty miles. I'd never been on so long a trip in my life. Sam used to go to help Father, and after Sam went off to college Father got Tom Warrups to go with him. But Tom was busy, and so this time Father had to take me.

Verplancks Point was on the Hudson River, just south of a town called Peekskill. Boats from New York City and Albany stopped there for trading. The idea of our trip was to drive cattle to Verplancks Point where we could sell them, and then use the money to buy supplies we needed for the tavern and the store— rum, cloth, pots and pans, needles and thread and all sorts of things. The traders brought these things up the river from New York and sold them to merchants at towns along the way, like Verplancks Point. And of course the merchants there wanted cattle to ship down to New York where there was a need for beef.

In October Father began gathering cattle. Some he got from farmers who paid their bills to him with cattle every year. Some he just bought, knowing he could sell them at a profit. It would take us three days to drive the cattle over and three days to come back. On horse-back you could ride it in a day, but we'd have not only the cattle but the wagon drawn by oxen with us. Going over we'd have a few pigs in the wagon; coming back we'd carry the things we bought in it.

On the way we'd stop at places where Father knew people. One night we would spend with those cousins of mine I'd never met. Father always stopped at the same places. They expected him every year: it was a good chance to catch up on family news.

The trip was planned for the end of November. It

was best to go as late in the year as you could, because the closer to winter it was, the scarcer beef was and the higher the price you could get. But if we waited too long, it would snow and then we would have trouble. Most of the time it was easier to travel when the snow was on the ground. You just hitched a horse to a sledge and slid over the packed snow. But it was hard to drive cattle in snow, and it was hard to pasture them along the way, too. So about the beginning of November Father began keeping a sharp eye out on the weather. He'd consult some almanacs, which usually disagreed, and he'd ask certain farmers who were supposed to be good judges of weather when they thought the snow would come. But the weather judges didn't agree any more than the almanacs did, so in the end Father would go out and frown at the sky a dozen times a day, and then make a guess.

The truth is that Father didn't really want to take me. "I don't think you're big enough yet to handle the wagon," he told me.

"I know how to handle the wagon, Father. I've done it lots of times."

"Around here, yes. But not with thirty cows to look after as well. Besides, the woods are full of those cow-boys over there. They claim they're patriots gathering beef for the troops, but really they're nothing more than thieves. And we don't have a gun anymore."

Father was right about the thieves who people called cow-boys. We'd heard all kinds of stories from travelers about them. All of that part of Westchester County, from the Connecticut border over to the Hudson River, had gotten to be a kind of no man's land, with roving bands wandering around plundering people on the excuse that they were part of the war. "I'm pretty brave, Father," I said.

He shook his head. "I don't like taking you, Tim, but I have no choice. There's nobody else to do it."

I was glad there was nobody else to do it. It was pretty boring hanging around the tavern day after day, making fires and chopping wood and cleaning up and looking after the chickens and Old Pru and the pigs. There would be a lot of exciting things on the trip—meeting my cousins and seeing the Hudson River which they said was a mile wide, and watching the boats sail up and down it. Besides it would get me out of school for a few days.

So Father collected cattle and watched the weather; and on the twentieth of November he came in from his weather look saying, "It's cloudy and getting chilly. I think we'd better start off in a day or two."

It was a good guess. When we started out two days later there was a half an inch of snow on the ground which had fallen during the night. The sun came up later on and melted it, making the roads muddy, especially after the cattle had churned it up. I walked alongside the wagon guiding the oxen and keeping them moving when they slowed down. We had four hogs in the cart, with their feet tied together. They were always trying to get out, and I had to make sure they didn't get loose. Father rode our horse Grey along behind the cattle to keep them moving. We went pretty slowly. There wasn't much to do except to look around at the hills and fields. It seemed pretty exciting when we passed a house, especially if there were some people there. A couple of times there were children staring out the windows as we went by. It made me feel proud of myself for being a man while they were still children, and I shouted at the oxen and smacked them on their rumps with my stick, just to show off how casual and easy I was with oxen and how used I was to managing them.

Father's plan was to go up through Redding Ridge to Danbury, and then turn a bit southward to go through Ridgebury and across the border into New York, where we'd spend the night in North Salem with our cousins. We'd spend the second night with friends of Father's at their farm near Golden's Bridge. It wasn't the straightest way over to Verplancks Point, but Father went that way because it took us past our cousins' place.

We reached Ridgebury around lunchtime. We didn't

stop to eat, but chewed on some biscuits and drank some beer for thirst as we walked along. We couldn't have a conversation, really: the cattle made too much noise as they tromped along mooing, and we had to shout to hear each other. And that was why we didn't hear the men riding up on us until they came in sight over a little hill in front of us.

There were six of them, and they were carrying weapons—mostly old muskets, but one or two of them had swords and pistols. They were dressed in ordinary clothing—brown shirts and trousers and muddy boots. As they came toward us, I began to turn the oxen to the side of the road so they could pass. But they didn't go on by. They charged up to us, surrounded us, and stopped. I knew they were cow-boys. I pulled the wagon's long brake lever and whoa-ed the oxen. The cattle stopped going forward and began milling around. I turned and looked back at Father.

He sat on his horse among the cattle looking very calm. "What's this?" he said.

One of the cow-boys pushed through the cattle to get close enough to Father to talk. "What's your name?"

"What business is it of yours?" Father said. I was hoping Father wouldn't argue with the man—it scared me.

"Government business," the cow-boy said.

"No doubt," Father said.

"Answer the question or we'll hang you and the boy from the nearest tree."

"My name's Meeker," Father said.

"Where from?"

"Redding."

"Redding?" The man turned in his saddle and spit onto the muddy road. "Tory country," he said. "I suppose this cattle is going to end up in Lobsterback stomachs."

Father shrugged. "Where it ends up I don't know and I don't care. I've been selling my beef at Verplancks Point for ten years, and I haven't yet asked who was going to eat it."

"Times have changed, Meeker. Now we want to know who's doing the eating. And we don't want it to be Lobsterbacks. There's only one place where beef goes from Verplancks Point and that's New York. And the British army owns New York."

I was getting pretty scared. He was tough-looking.

Father shrugged again. "I can't tell anybody what to do with a cow after I've sold it to him. That's his business."

"So the point then is not to sell it to the wrong people, isn't it?"

"I can't tell who—"

"Get down off that horse, Tory."

"I don't think I like being called that," Father said calmly.

"Please, Father," I said.

"Jesus," the cow-boy said. "All right if you don't want to get down from the horse, we'll knock you off it." He pulled a pistol from his belt and pushed his horse a few steps further until he was within reach of Father.

"Father," I shouted.

He grimaced and shook his head. Then he got down from the horse.

"That's better," the man said. "Now you and the boy walk out into the middle of that field and sit down."

I looked at Father. "Do what he says, Tim. Go out there."

"Aren't you coming?"

"Go, Tim."

By now the cattle were wandering around all over the place. Some of them had gone up the road ahead of the wagon. Others were edging out into the pastures alongside the road looking for forage. I pushed past a couple of cows, trotted out into the middle of the field, and sat down about fifty yards away from where Father was standing among the cows talking to the cow-boys. I knew he was trying to talk them out of taking the cows. If we lost our cattle, we'd be in a lot of trouble because we'd have no way of getting rum and the things we needed to run the store and the tavern.

I could see him gesturing—pointing up the road and then out to me as he explained something to the men. I wondered if he was scared. He seemed so calm and cool with the cow-boys, but I wondered if down underneath he was really scared. I knew I was scared.

Then I saw the man who had been doing all the talking lean down from the horse and hit Father with something—the barrel of his pistol I guessed. Father put his hands up to cover his head. The man hit him again and Father disappeared. He just dropped down among the cows and I couldn't see him anymore. I jumped up, but Father didn't get up and I still couldn't see him. "Father," I shouted. The cow-boys turned to look at me. "Please," I shouted. "Please don't hit him anymore."

The men turned away from me. The man who had hit Father got off his horse and stood there beside it, staring down at the ground. I knew he was looking at Father. He was still holding the pistol in his hand. "Please don't shoot him," I shouted. "Please."

This time they didn't even turn around to look at me. The man on foot kept waving the pistol around. He seemed to be talking, but I couldn't hear what he was saying. I stood in the middle of the field trying to think. Maybe I could run across the fields and find a

farmhouse where they might be able to get some people
to come and save Father. But if the cow-boys saw me
running, they could easily catch me in the open fields,
and ride me down if they wanted. I didn't know if I was
brave enough to take a chance. The cow-boys were still
looking down at Father. I turned and began to run across
the field. Behind me I heard somebody shout. Then I
heard horses galloping. I swirled around to look. The
cow-boys were galloping off down the road in the direction they had come from, leaving the cattle and the
wagon standing in the middle of the field. I stared;
and then a different group of riders came charging up
the road from the other direction. There were a dozen
of them, and they were driving hard. As they came up
to the cattle still milling about on the road they reined
up sharply. Then most of them threaded their way
through the cattle and dashed on, leaving two behind.
I saw Father stand up, and I began running back across
the road to the field.

The new horsemen had dismounted, and by the time
I reached Father, they were helping him to the side of
the road. I ran up. "Don't worry, Tim," he said. "I'm
all right."

He had a bad cut on his head which was still bleeding and another smaller one over his eye. His eye was
swollen and it was going to be black and blue by the
next day. He sat down on the ground while one of the

men washed the cut on Father's head with water from a leather canteen and bandaged it with Father's own handkerchief.

"Who were those people?" Father asked. "Cowboys?"

"Cattle thieves is a better name. We had reports that they were riding this morning, and we've been looking for them all day. You're a Loyalist, I take it?"

"I'm interested in making a living, not fighting a war," Father said. "My boy and I are just trying to get this beef to Verplancks Point the way I do every year."

"Verplancks Point?" The man grinned. "It'll go to New York, then. We'll see that it gets there. There are still a lot of people loyal to His Majesty in these parts."

So they did. They waited until the others gave up on the chase and came back, and then they rode with us to the New York line. We waited there again until they got us another escort to take us farther along the way, and we crossed over into New York, the first time I'd ever been in a colony besides Connecticut. It disappointed me. It didn't look any different and I didn't feel any different, either. Here I was in a foreign country, and it was just like being at home.

M Y NORTH SALEM COUSINS LIVED IN A CLAPBOARD
farmhouse just off the Ridgefield Road. Their name
was Platt and there were a lot of them—four girls and
two boys and the parents and their aunt who lived with
them, too. The house wasn't really big enough for
them. The four girls slept in one room with the aunt—
three girls in one bed and the biggest girl and the aunt

in another. The boys slept out in the barn except during the coldest weather, when they made up pallets on the floor in front of the kitchen fireplace. When I saw how crowded they were I realized that I was lucky not to have been raised on a farm: there was usually plenty of room in the tavern for me and Sam.

We got there after dark. They gave Father and me some bread and stew, and they all crowded into the kitchen to talk. It seemed like they all wanted to talk at once. They hadn't seen Father for a year and they wanted all the news: how Mother was and what the war was like in Redding and where Sam was and all the rest of it. They were curious about me—they'd been hearing about me for twelve years, and finally they were seeing me with their own eyes. And I'd been hearing about them all that time, too, and it was interesting for me to see them.

I felt shy, but they didn't because it was their house. So they began asking me a lot of questions until Mr. Platt made them all be quiet so he and Father could talk. Father told them about the scary thing that had happened on the way over.

Mr. Platt just nodded. He was a tall, thin man, and his clothes hung on him loosely. "They call themselves Patriots. They say they're only trying to keep people from selling beef to the British, but don't believe it. They'll take it and sell it to the British themselves if nobody else will buy. They're just cattle thieves." He was angry. "Lawlessness has run wild, common decency between people has disappeared, every man is armed against his neighbor."

"In Redding we still have law and order," Father said.

"We should have it here, too. There are plenty of Loyalists in Westchester County, but there's no control. Rebel and Tory live almost in open warfare with each other."

With hot food in my stomach and the open fire near-by, I was having a hard time staying awake. I knew I ought to go to bed because we had another hard day ahead of us, but I didn't want to miss the talk.

"I'm happy we haven't got to that point in Redding," Father said.

"You're fortunate. People have been tarred and feathered here, houses have been burned and livestock slaughtered. Both sides are doing it—one side burns a house and the other side retaliates. It won't be long before they're hanging people. I tell you it's true, Life."

"What about the party that escorted us here?"

"That's one of our Committees of Safety. They're about all we have to keep order. You were lucky—somebody along the way saw you pass by and knew there'd be trouble. There'll be trouble all the way to the Hudson."

My Father shook his head. "I suppose that next year I won't be able to get over here at all without an armed guard escorting me all the way."

"I judge you're right, Life."

My eyelids closed. I struggled to open them again, and then the next thing I knew Father was shaking me and saying, "Come on, Tim, time for bed."

My cousin Ezekiel Platt took me out to the barn. He was only a little older than me. He was tall and skinny like his father and had red hair. We climbed up into the loft, wrapped some hay up in blankets for pallets, and settled into bed. Ezekiel was curious about me and wanted to talk. "Were you scared when those men came?"

I didn't like to admit I was scared, but I didn't want to lie, either. "Some," I said. "Did you ever have that happen to you?"

"We haven't had any trouble yet, but Father says that's just because we've kept our noses clean. We don't make an issue of being Loyalists," he said.

"Are you a Loyalist?" I asked.

"Of course. Aren't you?"

"I guess so," I said. "Only sometimes I'm not sure. Sam's fighting for the Rebels, did you know that?"

"We heard that," Ezekiel said. "Father got into a rage. He said that Sam was too smart a boy to be fooled by sedition."

"He fought in the battle for New York," I said. "Father says he's headstrong, but he's very daring besides being smart."

"My father didn't think he was so smart for joining the Rebels. They're likely to be hung when the war's over."

"Maybe they'll win," I said.

"They can't. How can they beat the whole British army? It'll serve them right for being disloyal."

"Well I don't know," I said. "The way Sam explains it, it sounds right to be a Rebel. And when Father explains it, it sounds right to be a Loyalist. Although if you want to know the truth, I don't think Father really cares. He's just against wars."

We didn't say anything for a while. "If you go to be a soldier, which side would you fight on?"

"The loyalist, I guess." But in my head I wasn't sure about that. Suppose one day we were fighting and I suddenly saw that it was Sam I was aiming my gun at?

We woke up before the sun, hitched the oxen to the wagon, herded the cattle out of the Platt's pasture where they had spent the night, and started off again on the road toward Peekskill. Peekskill was on the Hudson River. We would turn south there and go down the river about five miles to Verplanks Point. From North Salem to Peekskill was more than twenty miles. It would take us all day to make fifteen miles to our next stop, Father's friends south of Mohegan. We were supposed to pick up another escort. I hoped we would find it soon. I didn't like traveling through this country alone, and I kept looking around all the time for galloping horsemen.

The escort picked us up at Purdy's Station. They stayed with us for about ten miles and then another escort took over. We spent the night with Father's friends, pasturing the cattle in one of their fields. In the morning another escort took us to Peekskill. It was a pretty big town—hundreds of people lived there. It was on the edge of the Hudson River, and as we rolled down the hill into the town we suddenly could see the water. I couldn't believe it—it was the biggest river I'd ever seen. Across the other side were beautiful hills, some of them craggy and rocky, dropping straight down to the water's edge. It was so beautiful I could hardly keep my eyes off it. "Father, it's so big," I said.

He grinned. "This is nothing, Tim. Wait till we get down to Verplanks Point. The river there is three miles wide."

The escort left us at Peekskill. We turned south, following a road that went along the river. Oh, it was exciting to me. There were all kinds of boats going up and down or moored offshore. Scattered along the river bank were docks and wharves with skiffs and rowboats tied up to them. Men and boys were fishing from the docks, and sometimes we could see people out in boats seining. It seemed like fun, a lot more fun than being a tavern-keeper.

"I wished we lived here, Father," I said.

He shrugged. "If wishes were horses beggars would ride."

"Still," I said.

"Oh, the river's pretty," he said, "but fishing's hard work. You try hauling one of those seines up from the bottom sometime and you'll find out."

"Are the people here Loyalists?"

"A mixture. The Dutch settled most of the land up and down the Hudson. There are a lot of them still here and they don't much care for the English crown."

We reached Verplancks Point at the end of the afternoon. It was a wedge-shaped spit of land which poked out into the river. Father had been right; the river was gigantic here. I could just barely make out the houses on the hillside across it they were so far away. It was like a huge lake filled with boats. "They call this part of the river Haverstraw Bay," Father told me.

At Verplancks Point the land was not steep, but sloped gradually down to the water. There was a long wharf jutting out into the river, with some boats tied to it. Set back on the land were pens for cattle, sheep and hogs; and around and about were sheds and houses belonging to the men who worked the docks and shipped the livestock. Most of it went down to New York. There were thousands of British troops quartered in New York, and British sailors, too, besides the regular population of 25,000. They needed as much beef as they could get and prices were going up all the time.

Father found Mr. Bogardus, the man he usually sold his livestock to. We herded the cattle into pens, and untied the poor hogs and turned them loose in the hog pens, too. Then Father said, "I'll be talking business with Mr. Bogardus for a while. Have a look around, but don't stray too far."

The sun was going down red and cold over the dark hills across the river. It felt good to be free of the animals. I had nothing to worry about for a while and that was nice. Going back would be easy with only the wagon full of goods to watch over. Of course there could always be trouble from the cow-boys, but Father didn't seem worried about it, so I put it out of my mind and wandered down to the wharf to see what was going on. The river was beginning to turn black, and the fishing boats were coming into the wharf. They tied up, and the men and boys in them handed out barrels of fish. I could see that Father had been right: they looked tired and wet and cold and dirty from the mud that came up from the bottom on the nets. One boy about my age got off a boat and just sat right down on the dock and stayed there, all huddled up under his coat, too tired to move.

They carried the fish into one of the sheds near the wharf and began to clean them. It was amazing to me to see how fast they worked—snap-snap-snap with a knife and there was the fish with its head slapped off and opened up into two white fillets. There were a lot of pretty big fish, too—sturgeon, they called it.

Finally I began to get cold myself and walked off the wharf and back up to the pens. It was warmer there by the animals, and after a while Father came along. We staked the oxen out in a bit of grazing common near the pens and went into the tavern for some supper. Father was happy. He had got a good price for the cattle and had negotiated for most of the other things he wanted to bring back to Redding. It was a good wagonload: two hogsheads of rum, a half dozen big sacks of salt, a couple of barrels of molasses; a large chest of tea, a sack of coffee beans, a dozen brass kettles and some tin pots; a chest of breeches and some brass buckles; some drills, knives, files, axes and spades; and small boxes of pepper, allspice, cinnamon, and white powdered sugar.

We slept that night in the tavern. "We ought to sleep in the wagon and save the money," Father said, "but I guess it's too cold for that."

The next morning we loaded the wagon with the things Father had bought and started off. Father tied the horse to the back of the wagon and walked along beside me to help manage the oxen. It was nice having company. I was sorry to say good-bye to the Hudson River. I liked being there and when we reached Peekskill and turned up the long hill away from it, I kept looking back over my shoulder at the water shining in the sun until we went over the brow of the hill and I couldn't see it anymore.

We spent the night at Father's friends near Mohegan. In the morning we got up at sunrise and left. The sky was cloudy and hung down over our heads like a blanket. "It's going to snow pretty soon," Father said.

"It's cold enough," I said.

"I think so," he said. "At night it will be, anyway. I hope we beat it home. I don't want to travel twenty miles with the oxen slipping and sliding up and down every hill." He shook his head. "We've got a problem, Tim. I want to avoid the Ridgebury area where we ran into those so-called Rebels before. I thought we'd curve south a little, hit into Connecticut at Wilton Parish and then go up through Upawaug to Redding, but that'll take us a half day out of our way, and with the snow coming, I'm not sure we want to risk it."

I didn't feel so easy when I thought about the cowboys. "Do you think they might be waiting for us?"

He shrugged. "They know we have to come back sometime. The people in Mohegan heard that a drover from Norfield had been shot on the Ridgebury Road two days ago and his cattle driven off."

"Was he killed?"

"Nobody knew. The report may not be reliable anyway." He shook his head. "I don't know, Tim, if it snows we ought to go the shortest way home, but I don't like going back through Ridgebury."

"If it's snowing really bad maybe the cow-boys won't want to come out raiding."

"There's that," Father said.

I didn't say anything more. Neither being raided nor traveling through the snow was going to be much fun. We just pushed on. There wasn't much to do; mostly I stayed at the head of the oxen and kept them moving. Sometimes Father walked with me, but sometimes he mounted Grey and rode on ahead a mile or so. He didn't tell me what he was doing, but I knew; he was scouting the road ahead for cow-boys.

It began to snow just after noon. It wasn't much at first—just a few light flakes drifting down from the sky. "Damn," Father said. "Oh damn."

"Maybe it'll stop," I said.

"No," he said, "we're in for it now."

We pushed on. Ten minutes later the sky was full of flakes falling quietly through the air. It was beginning to feel colder and every once in a while a quick gust of wind would slash the snow into our faces. "It's going to be a bad one," Father said.

"Maybe it'll pass by," I said.

"I'm afraid not, Tim." He frowned. "I think we'd better take a chance on going back by Ridgebury. I don't think many men will want to ride in deep snow."

By one o'clock it was a real, hard snowfall. The wind had picked up and the snow was blowing into our faces. The oxen became white and wet and they kept shaking their heads to throw the snow off. We walked along with our heads bent forward to keep the wind and snow from flying in our faces. I tucked my hands in my shirt for warmth.

In the middle of the afternoon we reached a fork in the road. "Hold up the oxen," Father said. I prodded them to a stop. He stood by the cart staring around him. There was already six inches of snow on the ground and it was blowing steadily down on us. "We could turn off here for Wilton Parish," he said. Then he shook his head. "There's no hope for it, Tim. We can't go on through this all night. We'll have to push on to North Salem and hole up at the Platt's until it stops, and then take our chances on Ridgebury."

I didn't feel very good. My hands were cold and my face was cold, and my feet were getting wet through my boots and they were going to be cold, too. I couldn't stop thinking about the cow-boys. We'd just been lucky getting away from them the first time. They were bound to be angry with us now for escaping, and they'd want to hurt us to get even. "Can we get an escort through Ridgebury, Father?"

"I don't know," he said. "We'll ask at the Platt's."

The walk seemed to go on and on. The oxen were

balking at walking in that blowing snow. They kept
trying to turn their backs to it, and it took Father walking on one side of them and me on the other to keep
them going straight. They blinked and shook their big
heads and bawled. It was queer how the heavy falling
snow muffled the sounds of their bawling. Fighting
them all the time was tiring. Several times they just
stopped and lowered their heads and stood blinking in
the snow, and it took us five minutes of beating them
and cursing them to get them going again. It seemed
to go on endlessly. With all that snow pouring down
around us I couldn't tell where we were. We could
only see about twenty yards in any direction—far
enough to tell when we might be passing a woodlot or
a house if it was close to the road, but that's all. But
Father always knew where we were. "Bear up, Tim,"
he'd say. "It's only a mile to Green's Tavern and just
three miles from there."

"Can we warm up at the tavern?"

"The fewer people who know we're going through,
the better," he said. I ducked my head against my chest
and tramped on.

It began to get dark. What with the oxen balking so
much we were two hours behind schedule. The snow
was almost a foot deep and already the oxen were having trouble on the hills, slipping and stumbling when
their hooves would strike an icy patch or a pothole
hidden beneath the snow. The darkness increased until

it seemed as if we were buried in it. I went on a couple of yards ahead of the oxen to feel out the road, while Father wrestled with them alone. We didn't talk anymore, except when Father cursed. Finding the road was hard. I would have to keep veering from side to side to touch the rail fences and then make a guess about where the middle of the road was. Looking back I could just make out the black lumpy shapes of the oxen and the cart, with Father fighting along at their heads. Once he said, "This is Simple's Crossing. Only two miles, Tim." Two miles seemed like an endless distance.

But finally we saw the spot of light and then the windows shining through the snow. We pulled the oxen through the gate and drove them into the barn. They bawled with happiness. Father went into the house to tell the Platts that we were there. I unhitched the oxen, pitched them some hay, and went into the house myself. There was a great fire burning in the kitchen fireplace and the smell of Johnny cake and hot gravy. My cousins swarmed around to help get my clothes off. I stripped right down to the skin, not caring that the girls were watching. They got me a blanket to wrap up in and a place by the fire and a plate of hot Johnny cake and beans and gravy all over it, and I began to laugh because it felt so good to be warm and safe again. That night my cousins and I slept by the kitchen fire.

IX

WHEN I WOKE UP IN THE MORNING IT HAD STOPPED
snowing and the sun was shining. Water was running
in small streams off the roof. It was pretty—everything
a foot deep in snow and the sun sparkling off the fields.
But even though it was pretty I didn't like it. Plowing
through snow a foot deep with the oxcart all the way
back to Redding was going to be miserable work. Our

feet would get soaked right away and stay wet and cold all day long, and as the snow got warm and then chopped up by the oxen we'd find ourselves stumbling around in a slippery mixture of snow and mud. Mrs. Platt gave us a breakfast of biscuits and gravy. We said good-bye to everybody, hitched up the oxen and pulled out of the yard onto the road. "Are we going to have an escort?" I asked Father.

"I don't know," he said. "Platt rode out last night to arrange for one, but with the snow, people may not want to ride. But that works two ways—the raiders may not want to ride, either. You work the oxen; I'm going to ride on ahead."

So that's how it went. Father would ride a mile or two and then ride back to see how I was doing; and then he'd ride out again. That way if he ran into the cow-boys he could race back to me and we could find a place to hide. "If you hear me shout, don't wait, run for the nearest piece of woods you see. They won't come into the woods on horseback in this snow."

The only trouble with this plan was that there usually weren't any woods close to the road. Most of the farmers had used up the trees near their houses and had their woodlots on back land. But still there were patches of woods here and there, so as I plowed along through the snow I kept looking around for woodlots to run to if something happened. It wasn't going to be easy running in that snow, though.

But there was nothing to do about it but push on. The oxen were more willing to pull than they had been the day before. It was warm enough and there was no snow blowing in their faces. But they kept slipping, especially on the hills, and I would have to tug and pull at them to keep them going forward.

I was alone most of the time because Father was out of sight somewhere up the road. In the snow Grey made very little noise, so that I couldn't hear him coming. Every once in a while Father would surprise me by riding silently into sight. He'd wave, and I'd wave back to let him know that everything was all right, and he'd ride away again.

I didn't like being alone so much. Suppose the cowboys came suddenly up behind me? Or suppose they were hiding in one of the houses or barns along the side of the road? They'd get to me before I could run. As I slogged along I kept turning around and looking down the road behind me, trying to see around corners and through clumps of trees. About every five minutes I would imagine that I was hearing horses, and jump around ready to run for it. Then I would look up and there would be nothing but the empty white sheet lying over the fields and hills.

At lunchtime Father came back. We sat in the wagon, drank some beer and ate some biscuits. "Ridgebury is about two miles up ahead," he said. "I'll ride through and come back and then we'll go through together. I'll be a lot happier when we're through this place." He shook his head. "We might as well push on and get it over with, Tim," he said. "Bear up, it won't last forever."

We got through Ridgebury all right. Some people came to the tavern door and stared at us as we went through. I guess they thought it queer to see us trying to travel in that snow. Father looked grim. "If nobody knew we were around before, they do now," he said. Then we got out of the village and he rode on ahead again, scouting.

My feet were wet and cold, and I was still hungry— biscuits and beer don't make much of a lunch when you're working oxen along. To keep my mind off my troubles I began trying to name all the countries in the world, which I was supposed to know because I'd learned them in geography. Some were easy to name: England, France, Sweden, Russia. But there were all those little hard ones, like Hesse and Tuscany and Piedmont. It took me a while to decide if I should count America or not. If the Rebels won the war then we would be a country; but Father was sure they were going to lose, so I decided not to count us. Another trouble was keeping them all straight in my head. After I got over twenty I'd sometimes forget whether I'd already counted Serbia or India or some place and have to go back over the whole list again. And I was trying to figure out whether or not I'd counted Arabia when it suddenly hit me that I hadn't seen Father for a long, long time.

I was shocked. How long had it been since the last time he'd ridden silently into sight? I couldn't tell. It seemed like it had to be a half an hour at least, and maybe an hour. I jumped up onto the wagon and looked back across the white countryside, trying to get a feeling of how far I'd come since I last saw him. All I could see was white, a few clumps of trees, a couple of farmhouses, and the muddy black trail of the oxcart winding through it. Where had I been when I last saw Father? I couldn't remember.

Maybe I was wrong. Maybe it had only *seemed* like a long time. Maybe being involved with listing all those countries gave me a funny idea of time.

But I didn't believe it; we'd come a long way, as far back over the hills as I could see, and that was a couple of miles. Now I was really worried. Of course there were a lot of simple explanations. Father could have met somebody he knew and started talking. Or he could have gone off somewhere to look for an escort. Or he could have stopped at a farmhouse to get us something warm to eat. There were a lot of explanations, but I knew none of them were true. If he'd been planning to leave me alone for a while he would have told me. He wouldn't have left me by myself this long; he just wouldn't have done it.

So then what? Perhaps something had happened to

Grey. He could easily have tripped in the snow and hurt himself. Maybe Father got hurt in the accident, too. Maybe he twisted an ankle or even broke his leg. No matter what it was, the important thing was for me to catch up to him quickly. I belted the oxen across their rumps with my stick. They grunted and shivered their heads and picked up their pace a little, but five minutes later they had slowed down. I hit them again, this time harder. They went faster but hardly for more than a minute or two. They couldn't go much faster because of the snow, and even if they could they just weren't going to. They weren't horses, they were oxen and they just plain didn't move fast.

That worried me some more. If Grey had slipped, Father might have been badly hurt. He might be bleeding or even lying unconscious in the snow. And to tell the truth, I was feeling scared and lonely without him. I wanted to find him. So I pulled the oxen as far off to the side of the road as I could, kicked away some snow so they could find some weeds to graze on, and started plowing on up the road as quickly as I could.

It was easy enough to follow Grey's tracks. Nobody else had been along the road but Father. It was hard trying to jog in the snow, and I began to sweat. Every few minutes I stopped to rest and have a look ahead. If there was a rock or a high stump by the roadside I would climb up on that and look on ahead. But all I saw were the horse tracks running on and on.

I went on along like this for around fifteen minutes covering a good mile and maybe more, when I saw a patch of hemlocks bordering the left-hand side of the road. There was a farmhouse on the hillside behind them. Perhaps Father had gone in there for food or something. I considered cutting off the road across the field to go directly to the farmhouse, but then I decided I'd better stick to following the horse tracks, in case. I plowed on until I came to where the hemlocks began to border the road, casting a cool shadow on the snow. There it was written out for me to see as plain as if I were reading it in a book. The road was all a turmoil of mud and snow marked with dozens of hoofprints. There were more hoofprints in the hemlock grove; and then going on up the road away from me the tracks of three or four horses. The cow-boys had lain in ambush in the hemlock groves, jumped Father, and taken him away someplace.

I stood there in the snow trying to think, but my mind just stopped working. All I could think was that Father was gone. I began silently to pray, "Oh please, God, oh please." Then suddenly I realized that the cow-boys might be still around, hiding somewhere and watching me. My neck began to prickle and I swung around and stared off across the fields, then back to the hemlocks. There was nobody. All was silence: no sound of horses, no sound of people talking, no sound of anything but a faint wind breathing in the tops of the hemlocks.

Why hadn't they come back for the wagon? Perhaps Father had got them to believe some story. Or perhaps they were going to do something with him first and then come after me and the wagon. What I wanted to do was start running and not stop until I got home. It wasn't more than twelve or fifteen miles: I could make it in three hours if I pushed. I was scared, that was the truth. It felt so lonely to be by myself with Father gone and maybe dead and nobody but myself to do—to do whatever had to be done. I was too scared even to cry; I just felt frozen and unable to move or think of what I should do next.

But finally I told myself that I had to stop being scared, I had to stop just standing there in the middle of the road. To get myself shaken awake I jumped up and down a few times and clapped my hands. That unfroze me a little and I began to think.

The first thing I did was duck back into the hemlocks to hide in case somebody came along. Then I asked myself what Sam would do if it were him, because he'd be brave and smart and do the right thing. And of course Sam wouldn't go running home. He'd do something daring. The most daring thing to do would be to track down Father, which wouldn't be too hard in the snow, and rescue him. That would be daring all right: I didn't have a gun, didn't have a sword or anything but a knife and a stick.

Then it came to me that even though rescuing Father was the daring thing to do, it wasn't the smartest thing. So I asked myself another question: what would Father do? And the answer that came pretty quickly was that he'd get the oxen and the wagon and the load of goods back home if he could so we'd have something to run the store and the tavern on through the winter. When I thought about it for a minute more I could see that it was the right answer. Maybe Father would get away; the cow-boys might even let him go after a while. One way or another he would be counting on me to get the wagon home—that was for certain.

I jumped out of the hemlock grove and started jogging back toward the wagon. The oxen wouldn't have strayed; oxen don't wander when they're attached to a heavy wagon. The only risk was that somebody had come along and stolen them or made off with the goods. I went along as fast as I could, all the while looking around for signs of people; but there was nobody and in a few minutes I got back to the wagon. Everything was all right. I picked up my stick, banged the oxen on their rumps and they heaved and grunted and started off.

There wasn't much point any longer in listening for

the cow-boys. I was pretty certain they'd be along sooner or later, after they'd done—done whatever they were going to do with Father. What I had to do was figure out some way of persuading them to leave me and the wagonload alone. I could always run up into the fields and save myself, but the point was to try to get the wagon home so we could earn our livelihood through the winter.

About half an hour later I came to the hemlock grove and the place along the road where they'd captured Father. Now I began to watch ahead for tracks leading off to the sides of the road where cow-boys might try to ambush me. But I didn't see anything, and on I went, trying to think of a good story for the cowboys when they came.

The sun was beginning to get down in the sky behind me. It would be getting dark soon. Already it was getting cold and a bit of a chill wind was springing up. I was just as glad of the dark, though. There were houses to pass by and little villages to go through and in the dark it would be safer. I planned not to stop for the night, but just push on all the way home. Besides, I didn't know of anyplace to stop; Father had friends along the way but they were strangers to me. I went on thinking about something to tell the cow-boys; and after a while I began to get an idea.

On I went, belting the oxen when they slowed down.

The sun dropped behind the hills in back of me, leaving a red smear on the sky, which slowly turned black. I shivered. I was hungry. There were some more biscuits and jerked beef in a sack in the wagon, and a bottle of wine Mr. Bogardus had given Father for a present. The wine would warm me up a bit. But I decided not to eat or drink anything yet. I knew I was going to be really tired and cold and miserable soon enough, and it would be nice to have the food and the wine to look forward to.

I was thinking about the wine when I saw the cowboys. They were sitting on horseback in the middle of the road about twenty yards ahead of me—three black figures stock still in the night. The sight of those unmoving figures shocked me, and I almost ran. But I didn't. Instead I slapped the oxen on their rumps as if I hadn't any worries about who was standing in the middle of the road. One of the horses stamped and his bridle jingled in the night.

I cleared my throat quietly so I wouldn't sound scared. Then I shouted, "Are you the escort? Am I ever glad to see you."

One of them pulled the cover off a lantern he had been holding. A circle of hazy light spilled out into the night, showing bits of horses and faces and guns and the trampled snow. "Pull up the oxen," the man with the lantern shouted.

I stopped the oxen up and walked forward a few paces. Then the man with the lantern leaned forward to let the light shine on me. "It's the boy," he said.

"Yes, sir," I said. "Father said that the escort would be along soon, but when you didn't come I was worried that the cow-boys would get to me first."

"We're not the——" one of them started to say.

"Shut up, Carter," the man with the lantern said. "Come here, boy."

I took a couple of steps forward. Now the lantern was shining in my eyes, and it was hard for me to look up and see their expressions. All I could see was the horses' legs and the snow. The man's voice just came out of the glare. "When did your father say the es— we'd be here?"

"He figured you'd be here an hour ago. That's why I was so worried. He told me not to worry, but I couldn't help it. He said that when the shooting started to fall flat and I'd be all right." I paused. "I thought there'd be more of you, though. Father said there'd be at least a half dozen men in the escort. He said just fall flat when the shooting started."

There was silence and then one of the others said, "I don't like this. It sounds like an ambush."

The man with the lantern swung around a bit to face him. "Are you going to get scared off by a boy's story?"

"What, sir?" I said.

"Never mind, boy."

"Do you have anything to eat, sir?"

"Shut up, boy."

"I don't like this. Let's go."

The man raised the lantern to look at the others. Now I could see their faces a little. Oh they looked tough—unshaven and dirty, wearing swords and pistols, and muskets tucked in behind their saddles. "Are both of you going to be scared off by a boy's story?" he snarled.

"I still don't like it. How do you know it's a story?"

"Oh stop being a couple of old women."

"It isn't worth the risk, Judson. Let's leave."

"Not worth the risk? There's a hundred pounds worth of stuff in that wagon."

"Judson, stealing rum is a hanging matter. I don't want to—"

Just then a dog barked in the distance. The oxen bawled.

"Damn," one of them said.

"It's them."

"It's just a dog barking," Judson shouted.

"I'm not taking the chance." He wheeled his horse in the snow, and the other did likewise.

"Damn you men," Judson said. But they had begun to gallop off through the snow. Snarling, he pulled the cover over the lantern, and then he wheeled his horse, too, and disappeared down the road.

I stood for a moment listening to the sound of their

hooves dying out in the snowy road, and then I began to laugh and cry all at once. My hands shook so hard I dropped my stick and my knees were so weak I could hardly walk. I felt terrific, because I'd fooled them; it would be a great story to tell Sam. But everything else was awful—Father being gone and me being alone in the snow and dark and hours to go before I got home.

I climbed into the wagon and ate the biscuits and beef and drank about half the bottle of wine. I guess I was sort of drunk, because I just kept putting one foot in front of the other and by midnight I was home.

HAVING FATHER GONE WAS STRANGE. THE TAVERN seemed cold and empty, the way it is when you wake up at night and realize that the fires have gone out. Mother didn't cry, except right at the beginning, the night I told her what had happened. She went on believing that he was alive. "They had no reason to kill him, Timothy. I believe they're holding him somewhere. They'll let him go by and by." But the days passed and he didn't come home, and soon she changed her story. "He's in a prison ship somewhere," she said. "As soon as this terrible war is over he'll come home again."

I didn't know whether she was saying what she believed or was just trying to keep me from thinking that my father was dead. Now half the family was gone and our lives were really changed. Mother and I had all the work to do, which meant that there was hardly any time off for either of us. We even had to work on Sunday, which was a sin. "God will forgive us, Tim," Mother said. "Don't worry about it, I'm sure of that." I didn't tell her that I wasn't worried.

But the work worried me all right. There was so much to do—old Pru and the chickens and sheep to take care of and the spring, planting the corn and greens we needed for the tavern, and the cleaning and the cooking. And of course somebody had to be at the tap all the time to draw beer and serve the meals to travelers and make up beds for people who came through needing a place to sleep. There were a lot of people going through, too—messengers going here and there and people moving to different towns and commissary officers and such. So business seemed good, but actually it wasn't, because a lot of people—the ones on official business—paid in commissary notes which were just pieces of paper that wouldn't be worth anything at all unless the Rebels won. You couldn't buy very much with the commissary notes: a lot of people wouldn't take them, unless they were strong Patriots and felt they ought to in order to show faith in George Washington and the Rebel government.

Business was good in the store, too. Food was in short supply and so was everything else, and we could sell anything we could get our hands on—cloth, farming tools, wheat, sugar, rum, anything at all. We even started dealing in used goods. Farmers were desperate for everything—shovels, plowshares, candle molds, churns, and all the rest of it. Sometimes Mother would hear of a widow whose husband had died or been killed in the war, and couldn't manage the farm anymore. She'd be willing to sell us the old farming tools, and we could easily resell them at a good price.

But even that didn't help much. Prices kept going up and up, and depreciation of the paper money took a lot of the profit out of it. You'd sell a bag of nails for a shilling, and when you went out to buy some more you'd find that the price had gone up to two shillings. So you came out behind. We'd raise the price of nails and then by the time we were able to get hold of anymore the price would have gone up again, and we'd still be behind. Of course you weren't supposed to raise prices. The Connecticut General Assembly had made laws about how much you could charge for things. But the laws weren't any use: if you had to pay two shillings for nails, you couldn't sell them for two shillings, no matter what the law said. What we did was get around the law by charging the legal two shillings for the nails, or whatever it was, and then charge a shilling more for the bag we sold them in. It wasn't really honest, but we didn't have any choice. The whole thing really made me feel pretty sick, working that hard from sunrise to sunset and never being able to get ahead. But there was nothing we could do about it except to pray every night that the war would end soon, and Father and Sam would come home again.

We spent a lot of time trying to get letters to Sam. Mother figured that once Sam realized that his own side had captured or maybe even killed his father he'd come home and help manage things. "He should be tired of playing soldier boy by now," Mother said. "I should think that glory would have worn off." She had a talk with Colonel Read about it. Colonel Read had been head of a whole regiment of militia, but he'd quit the job. He said it was because he was too old, but everybody knew that was just an excuse: he'd quit because he was against the war and didn't want to fight in it. He was a Patriot, but he didn't approve of the war.

He said to my mother, "Mrs. Meeker, even if you can persuade him to come home, they may not let him."

"That doesn't seem right."

"Of course Sam could claim it was a hardship case—
the father gone and only the younger brother left at
home. But the fact that Mr. Meeker is considered a
Tory won't help."

Mother said, "If he's got the brains he was born with
he won't tell them that, will he, Colonel Read?"

Colonel Read smiled. "I don't imagine he will, Mrs.
Meeker."

But I wasn't so sure anybody was going to be able to
change Sam's mind to begin with. He'd got himself set
to win the war and throw the British out of the country
so we could be free, and when Sam was determined he
usually stuck to things. Pigheaded was what some people called him, but not me. Of course I still hadn't
figured out what he was fighting for. It seemed to me
that we'd been free all along. What had the English
government ever done against me? I thought about
that a lot, and I never could find any way they'd hurt
me that had mattered very much. Naturally in church
we had to pray for the King and Parliament and that
was a nuisance because it made the prayers go on
longer. As a matter of fact, we weren't supposed to pray
for the King and Parliament anymore. The Assembly
had declared that it was treason to pray for them. But
Mr. Beach was pretty brave even though he was over
seventy-five years old, and he went on praying for

them anyway. A couple of times Rebels had come into the church and pulled him down from the pulpit and pushed him around, but he didn't care. He made us pray for the King and Parliament just the same.

Still, besides having extra prayers I couldn't think of anything the King had made me do that I didn't want to. But that wasn't the way Sam felt about it, and I wasn't exactly sure he'd come home even when he finally found out that Father was gone. There was only one way to find out, so we kept trying to get messages to him. We asked Betsy Read to tell him about Father if she got in touch with him, but she didn't know where he was anymore than we did.

So there were a lot of changes in our lives, but the biggest was the one that was happening inside myself. Ever since I had got the wagon home by myself I hadn't felt like a boy anymore. You don't think that things really happen overnight, but this one did. Of course I was dead tired when I went to bed that night, and Mother let me sleep late in the morning. And when I woke up I was different. I noticed it first at breakfast. Usually I sat there over my porridge moaning to myself about the chores I had to do or having to go to school or something, and trying to think of some way to get out of whatever it was. Or when Mother turned her head I'd scoop up a fingerful of molasses from the jar and stir it into my milk. Or I'd eat breakfast slowly so I could stall off going to work.

But that morning after the terrible trip home, right from the first moment we got finished saying grace, I began planning the things I had to do—which things had to be done first and what was the best way to get them done. It was funny: it didn't even cross my mind to stall or try to get out of the work. I didn't wait for Mother to tell me what to do: I brought the subject up myself. "I've got to get the wagon unloaded right away," I told her. "Everything will get damp sitting out there in the barn. Maybe I can get Jerry Sanford to help me roll the barrels down."

Mother nodded. I think she must have been surprised to hear me talk like that, but she didn't let on. "You'll need somebody bigger than Jerry. Perhaps you can hire Sam Smith's Negro, Ned."

We discussed it all, and about halfway through breakfast I began to realize that I had changed. I wasn't acting my usual self, I was acting more like a grownup. You couldn't say that I was really an adult, but I wasn't a child anymore, that was certain. I thought about showing off in front of Sam when he came home. I'd say things like, "Well, Sam, we've decided not to put in oats this year, we're going to use the space for corn." Or, "We're not keeping the kitchen fire going all the time—I haven't got enough time for woodcutting as it is." I would be the one who knew about things, not him.

But even though it was nice to feel more grown-up

and act that way, too, I missed Father. Especially toward the end of the day, when I was tired and cold and
hungry and there was still wood to be brought up and
the barn to be cleaned and Old Pru to be milked, I'd
begin feeling sorry for myself and wishing that Father
was back. I'd imagine that if I looked up I'd suddenly
see him striding into the barnyard, and I'd look up, but
he wouldn't be there. I'd stand there feeling disappointed, even though I'd really known he wouldn't be
there, and I'd get angry with the Rebels for starting
the war and angry with Sam for going to play soldier
and have the glory while I had to do all the work at
home. It wasn't fair. It would make me curse and I
didn't care whether cursing was a sin.

Winter came and winter went, and the war went on
in the same distant way. Oh, the effects of it were real
—the rising prices, the shortage of everything, the
news that so-and-so had been killed in some faraway
battle. But all the things you think of as belonging to a
war, the battles and cannons firing and marching troops
and dead and wounded—we hadn't seen any of it, except for the messengers and commissary officers who
came by.

It got to be the spring, 1777. The work went on,
except that instead of cutting wood, cleaning the barn
and pitching hay for the animals, I now spent my day
digging and planting in our kitchen garden by the side

of the house, so we'd have fresh vegetables for the tavern. And I was doing this one Saturday morning early toward the end of April—the 26th, to be exact—when I began hearing from a long way away a heavy muttering noise. It sounded a bit like thunder, but not exactly. It made me uneasy. I jammed the spade in the ground and went out front of the tavern to have a look up and down the road. The sound seemed to be coming from the southwest over behind the church somewhere, but there wasn't anything to be seen. And then I saw Ned, Samuel Smith's Negro, come running up the road. At the same moment Captain Betts popped out of his house next door. Captain Betts was in the Rebel militia. "What is it, Ned?" he shouted.

"British troops, Captain," Ned shouted. He ran on by.

Captain Betts turned back in the doorway. "Jerry," he shouted. "Quick, get Mr. Rogers here." Jerry Sanford dashed past him through the door and up the road toward the Rogers'. Captain Betts continued to stand there for a moment more, listening.

"What do you think they're doing, Captain Betts?" I called.

He looked grim. "It won't be anything good. There are a lot of them."

"Is the militia going to try to stop them?"

He scowled. "There aren't enough Patriots in Redding to stop a pair of cows going through." Then he went back into the house.

I turned and went into the tavern. Mother was scouring some pots. "British troops coming," I told her. "What do you think they'll do?"

"Drink and not pay for it," she said. "That's the rule with soldiers. Take the good pewter out to the barn and hide it in the hay."

I did it, and then I ran back around to the front to watch the soldiers come. Now I could see a fine shading of dust in the air out behind the church, rising slowly and drifting away. The noise grew louder. I watched, and all at once through the hedgerows I caught a glimpse of movement and things flashing. In a moment the vanguard appeared around the bend. There was a drummer boy banging away in front, and a standard bearer, and then a couple of officers on horseback, and then the marching men. On down the road toward me they came. It was a frightening thing to see. They just kept coming on and on as if nothing in the world could stop them.

Now I could see cannons, each of them about twelve feet long and drawn by two horses. I figured they must be six-pounders, from what I'd read about it. Behind them were wagons full of boxes and bags—powder and balls and such, I figured. The dust rose up through everything, turning the red uniforms, the cannons, the wagons all a greyish brown. They marched past the tavern, pulled off onto the training ground, and broke formation. Mr. Rogers ran by with Jerry Sanford coming behind him as fast as they could. They dashed into Captain Betts' house. I hoped they weren't trying to get the trainband organized to fight the British. That was impossible: there were hundreds of Redcoats milling around on the training ground—maybe thousands, even.

Most of the people in the village were standing in their yards, watching. The children kept dashing up the road to the training ground to get a closer look, until their mothers saw them and dragged them back home again. In the training ground the soldiers were settling down to eat breakfast, dumping their packs on the ground, and stacking their muskets into neat little tepees, four or five together. I kept hoping that some officers would come into the tavern for rum or beer or something to eat. I wanted to see them close up and listen to them talk. Oh, those troops were impressive-looking with all those belts and buckles and powder horns and bayonets and so forth dangling about their red uniforms. How could people like Sam expect to beat them?

But the officers didn't come into the tavern; instead, three or four of them rode up to Mr. Heron's house. I saw Mr. Heron open the door to let them in and they disappeared. I guessed that Mr. Heron had known in advance that they were coming. Probably he had set out a big breakfast for them. It gave me a funny feeling to realize that while Mr. Heron was giving the British officers rum and beef, Captain Betts and Mr. Rogers were sitting in the Betts' house a hundred yards away trying to figure out a way to kill them.

I went on watching. Some of the bigger children had got away from their mothers and were standing at the edge of the training ground, looking at the soldiers. After a while the children began shouting questions at the men like had they ever killed anybody and weren't they afraid of the Rebels and so forth. The soldiers joked back with the kids and after a while I walked over myself and listened.

"Where are you headed for?" I asked one of the Redcoats.

"If I knew I wouldn't tell yer." He had a funny accent.

"Where are you from?" I asked.

"Where are *you* from, lad?"

"Right there." I pointed to the tavern.

"Well I'm from old Dublin," he said. "And I wisht I was back there roight naow, 'stead of marching through this bloomin' place."

"What's Ireland like?"

"Oh, 'tis a lovely place, all green and cool like—if

you don't mind a spot of rain. How is it yer not afroid of us, you tykes?"

"We're mostly Tories here." Suddenly I realized that I was. Father's capture had done that.

"Ah," he said.

And I would have talked with him some more, but just then an officer came riding and shouted, "Get along you bloody Yankee scum. Back to your mothers." He slapped his quirt on his leg and we all ran.

I stood in our yard, watching. The officer shouted something to the soldiers. There was a scurrying around and then eight of them snatched up their guns, formed up into twos, and marched out behind the officer. He wheeled his horse about and trotted toward me. I jumped back and plunged for the tavern doorway. He galloped across our yard into the Betts' yard, pulled the horse up, and shouted some more orders. The soldiers charged for the Betts' door, bashed it open with the butt ends of their rifles, and slammed into the house. Five minutes later they came out again, pushing in front of them Captain Betts, Mr. Rogers, and Jerry Sanford. Jerry was dead white. He was trying not to cry, but the tears were squeezing out of his eyes and he kept wiping his face with his sleeve. The soldiers pushed the three of them onto the road, tied their hands behind their backs, and marched them onto the training ground through the troops. I knew now what the officers had gone up to Mr. Heron's for: it wasn't breakfast, it was to find out who the Rebel leaders were.

Now my mother was standing in the doorway beside me. "The brutes," she said. "What do they want with that little one? Can they think he's dangerous?"

"What are they going to do with them, Mother?"

"God have mercy on them," she said. "God have mercy on William Heron."

"They wouldn't shoot Jerry, would they?"

"War turns men into beasts. It's cheaper to shoot a boy than to feed him."

"I don't think they would, Mother. I don't think they'd shoot Jerry." It seemed unbelievable, but it made me go cold all the same.

She shrugged. "Maybe not. Only the Lord knows about that. Come into the house before they take a fancy to you. Who knows what Mr. Heron's told them about your brother."

"I'm all right, Mother."

"Come into the house, Timothy. I've lost two, I'm not losing another."

I went in. I was full of all kinds of funny feelings. At first when the troops had arrived, swaggering around so bold and gay, I had really admired them. But seeing them take Jerry Sanford off like that gave me a sick feeling in my stomach. I didn't think they'd shoot him. I figured they'd taken him away just be-

cause he lived with Captain Betts and happened to be
there when the soldiers had come. But still, maybe they
would shoot him. Maybe they'd want to torture him
for secrets or something—after all, he lived with one
of the Rebel leaders and might know what their plans
were or whether they had ammunition stored someplace.

I stood at the window watching. Mother told me to
get away from the window and go about my work, but
I didn't. I stayed there. Finally, about a half an hour
later, the officers mounted their horses and began riding through the troops shouting orders. Within a
couple of minutes the soldiers were formed up in the
training ground ready to march. And just as they were
about to start off there came the sound of a horse galloping. I dashed outside in time to see a horseman
come over the rise of the road from the direction of
Danbury. He was dressed in ordinary clothes, and I
guessed that he was a Rebel messenger. Suddenly he
spotted the British troops formed up on the training
ground. He reined up and wheeled the horse around.
Bending low, he kicked his heels into the horse and
started to tear off back the way he'd come. There was a
commotion in the British ranks, and a quick fusillade of
shots. The man suddenly straightened up in the saddle
and flung his arms out. His head jerked backwards, and
he slid off the back of the horse and lay still in the

dusty road. A British officer shouted, and the troops marched out. The rider's horse was cantering off in a field, bucking. The troops marched past the body. None of them turned to look at him. Finally the last of the wagons disappeared around the bend, and I started running down the road toward the body, scared of what I might see. Other people came running up, too.

The man was lying on his stomach with his face turned sideways. There was a tear in his shirt in the center of his back and blood was soaking through the cloth, but sweat was running off his pale face and he was breathing hard. "Pick him up and carry him to the tavern," Mr. Read said. "Meeker, go up to Doctor Hobart's house and tell him we've got a wounded man down here."

It was over two miles up to Dr. Hobart's. For a moment I thought about saddling up a horse, but the British troops were marching ahead of me in the direction of Dr. Hobart's, and I was afraid that if I came galloping by on a horse, they'd take me for a messenger and shoot me, too. On foot I could cut through the fields if I had to.

I began running. Within five minutes I ran into a dusty haze kicked up by the troops, and I realized that they must be just ahead of me. I jumped to the side of the road, swung over the stone wall, and cut across the pasture to the next stone wall, which was bordered by a line of trees. I slid over this wall and began running along it, parallel to the road. I figured out I would run past the British troops and come out ahead of them before they reached Dr. Hobart's house. It would take some running, though. The British column was a mile long.

I ran on, stumbling through the pasture stubble and furrows of the plowed fields. And I had covered almost two miles when I heard shots—at first only one or two, but then a fusillade. I dropped flat behind the stone wall and then raised my head to stare around. I couldn't see anything but the empty field that lay between me and the road. I slid over the stone wall and began to run crouched over toward the stone wall at the other side of the field which bordered the road. When I got to the wall, I flung myself flat and listened. The shooting was going on down the road a way. I took a chance and raised my head to look over the wall.

The British column was disappearing around the bend, but a couple of dozen troops had stayed behind. They were kneeling on the road in a line firing at Captain Starr's house across the road from them—on the other side from where I lay. From where I was hidden behind the stone wall I could look through the downstairs windows in the side of the house There were Rebels in there, firing back at the Redcoats. The way I figured it, the Rebels had hidden there and begun shooting at the British troops as they marched by. Through the windows I could see the Rebels moving around. I couldn't recognize all of them, but I knew some. One was Captain Starr. Another was Samuel Smith's Negro slave, Ned—the same one who'd first come running to report that the British were coming.

As I watched, one of the British pitched over flat on the road. The rest went on firing into the building, as if the bullets coming out at them didn't matter. It was the way the British fought.

Suddenly an officer shouted an order. The British troops rose, their bayonets flashing at the ends of their muskets. The officer raised his sword and charged toward the house, and troops ran after him. When they reached the door the officer stood aside while the soldiers battered the door with their muskets. Suddenly it crashed open, and the troops charged in. I heard somebody shout, "There are some damned blacks in here, what shall we do with them?"

"Kill them," the officer yelled. He charged through the door waving his sword. I could see Ned swivel away from the window where he crouched, attempting to swing his rifle around to get in a shot at the officer. But the officer was quicker. He slid his sword into Ned's stomach, and then jerked it free. Ned staggered around, still raising his gun up for the shot. The sword flashed in a bright arc, the fastest thing I ever saw move. Ned's head jumped off his body and popped into the air. I never saw it fall. I dropped down behind the stone wall and vomited all over myself. Then I got up and ran across the field and fell over the other stone wall. I lay there smelling my vomit and seeing Ned's head jump into the air. It was a long time before I realized that I was soaked with cold sweat and crying. I knelt up and listened. The shooting had stopped. I remembered the man in the tavern. He was dying, too, and I didn't want to have his death laid on me. I slipped along the hedgerow and when I was well past Starr's house I came up the field and back onto the road. For a moment I looked. In the distance I could see the British troops milling around the house. They were carrying heavy objects into the house. I knew what they were, but I didn't want to think about it. When the British had all the things in the house, they set the house on fire. I turned and ran down the road toward Dr. Hobart's. I didn't feel much like being a Tory anymore.

Dr. HOBART SADDLED UP AND RODE DOWN TO THE
tavern, and I walked back slowly. There wasn't any
hurry now. Mostly I tried to put out of my mind what
I'd seen. I went out to the barn and cleaned myself up
as best I could, and then I went into the taproom. It
was full of people who'd come to talk about the British
raid.

The wounded man was still alive. The ball had hit him high in his ribs and had stuck there without damaging him much. Dr. Hobart gave him a huge mug of rum, and when he'd drunk that down and it had had a chance to work, four men held the man down flat on a table while Dr. Hobart sliced open the wound and pulled the ball out with his forceps. "A couple of broken ribs," he said, "but they'll knit." He bound the man tightly, and we propped him up with some comforters in front of the fire and gave him some more rum and something to eat. He was pretty drunk, but he told us his story.

"They're after the munitions stored in Danbury," he said. "I came up here to warn the militia. We thought somebody might stop them. But I was too late."

Dr. Hobart shook his head. "A wasted errand," he said. "The trainband is pretty thin here."

"I know," the wounded man said. "But we were expecting some Continental troops. You've heard of General Benedict Arnold, I expect? He and General Silliman and some others have been chasing the British up from Compo in Fairfield. They were hoping somebody would slow them down until they could catch up. Although I don't know what good it would do, they haven't got the men to take on that bunch of Lobsterbacks."

I took a deep breath. Sam was with Benedict Arnold's troops. Or at least he had been. "Sir, you mean General Arnold's troops are coming through Redding?"

"That was the plan. Of course you can't ever tell what's going to happen in war. Things change a lot."

I knew it was foolish to believe that Sam might be with General Arnold's troops, but when you want something bad enough you can't stop yourself from hoping. I wondered if Mother remembered that Sam was with Arnold. I didn't think she would. She wouldn't have paid any attention to something like that.

I went to the window and looked out. It had clouded over and was beginning to rain. A man was running across the training ground. In a moment I saw that it was Captain Betts. He came swiftly toward the tavern, opened the door and came in.

"Stephen," somebody said. "You escaped?"

"They let some of us go," he said.

"How many?"

"Nine. They let most of us go. They only kept three."

"Is Jerry Sanford all right, sir?"

He shook his head. "They kept him. Don't ask me why they kept a boy."

"They kept Jerry? What will they do with him, sir?"

[148]

"I don't know," he said gruffly. "What's happened here?"

"They've gone off north toward Danbury," somebody told him. "They burnt Starr's house and killed some people there."

"Dan Starr? They killed Dan Starr?"

"Yes."

Captain Betts looked grim and hard. "The bastards. We can still catch them. I'm going to get the trainband out. We'll follow them through the fields and cut them down from behind the walls. Tim, go over and ring the church bell. Get cracking."

I didn't want to get into it, but I had to obey. I started toward the door, but my mother grabbed my collar. "No, no," she said. "Not my boy. You don't involve anymore Meekers in this terrible war. Send your own child out to play soldier if you want, Stephen Betts, but no more of mine."

Betts stared at Mother. "Where's your patriotism, woman?"

"Bah, patriotism. Your patriotism has got my husband in prison and one of my children out there in the rain and the muck shooting people and likely to be dead any minute, and my business half ruined. Go sell your patriotism elsewhere, I've had enough of it."

"They're killing your neighbors, Susannah," Captain Betts shouted. "They've killed Dan Starr."

"Then there's enough dead already."

"Tim—" he started.

Mother snatched up the poker from the fireplace. "Leave my boy alone, Stephen Betts," she said. She raised the poker over her head, and I knew from the mad look in her eye that she would hit Captain Betts if she had to.

"Mother," I said.

"The devil on you," Betts said. "I can't fool with you any longer." Then he turned and strode out of the tavern, banging the door behind him. A few minutes later the church bell began to toll the alarm. The people in the tavern began to leave. Some of them, I knew, belonged to the trainband and were going off to get their weapons. A lot of the others just smelled trouble and wanted to get clear of it. Pretty soon there were only a couple of men left. The wounded man had fallen asleep by the fire. Outside, the wind had begun to blow the rain against the windows. Night was falling.

Mother sat down at the table and put her head in her hands. "Timothy, I want to pray. Come here and pray with me." She took my hand and pulled me down on the bench beside her. I put my head down. "Oh Lord," she said, "please take this war away from here. What have we done to endure this? Why must it go on so long? What have we done in Thy sight to deserve this evil?" She stopped: but there was no answer and after a moment she raised her eyes, got up, and began to slice some onions into the stew pot for supper.

And an hour later, as I was getting hungry and wondering when supper would be ready, we heard distant sounds again—the sounds of marching men and horses trotting and orders being shouted. I looked at Mother. The wounded man by the fire raised his eyes. "They're coming back again," he said.

"Maybe it's the trainband," I said. But my heart was pounding, and I knew who I hoped it was. I ran out into the yard. It was nearly full dark, and the rain spattered in squalls against my face. I looked down the Fairfield Road. It was hard to make out much, but indistinctly I could see a body of men coming toward us. I pulled back into the shadow of the house, and watched them come up. After a while I began to make out the shapes of the ones on horseback. I could tell by their hats that they weren't Redcoats. I darted back into the tavern. "They're Continentals," I said.

"Thank God," the wounded man said.

Mother and I went to the window. The troops marched by, then broke formation, and began to spread out through the village looking for shelter from the rain. A lot of them went into the church or Mr. Heron's barn out behind. Then the tavern door banged open, and four or five men strode in. Leading them was a general, wearing the long blue Continental coat and cockaded hat with feathers in it. He said nothing to us, but dropped down at the table. The aides stood around him. "Rum for General Wooster, boy," one of the aides said. Then he looked at Mother. "You're the taverner, m'am?"

"Yes, sir."

"We'll need some dinner."

There went my stew. But I didn't care. General David Wooster was head of the Connecticut militia. I'd never seen a general up close before, and as I brought the rum and water I looked him over. I was disappointed: he wasn't very glorious-looking—just a tired old man who was worried and frowning. As I stared he yawned and rubbed his eyes. "Timothy," Mother snapped. "Bring the gentlemen their dinners."

Suddenly the wounded man began to struggle to his feet, and saluted.

"Who are you?" General Wooster said.

"Private Hodge, sir. I took a British ball this afternoon."

"They were here, then?"

"Yes, sir. They've gone on toward Danbury about eight hours ago."

General Wooster ran his hand across his eyes. "Eight hours," he said softly. "Damn." He took his hand off his eyes. "Sit down, sir," he said. "Was there any attempt made to stop them?"

The wounded man struggled to the floor. "No, sir. Not that I could see, sir."

I stepped forward. "Sir, some of the trainband fired

on them from a house just down the road. The Redcoats killed them all and burned Starr's house." I remembered Ned's head jumping off his shoulders.

"How many men in the house, son?"

"I don't know, sir. Maybe five or six."

Suddenly the door banged open again. Another Continental officer stood there, gazing around the room.
Then he walked in, followed by his aides, and crossed
the room to General Wooster. In a moment I saw the
insignia on his shoulder. He was a general, too. He
walked over to General Wooster, followed by his aides.
General Wooster got up. "Ben," he said. "It's good to
see you. Boy, a glass of rum for General Arnold."

So General Arnold was in Redding. I brought the
rum, and water and some bread, and we scraped out the
bottom of the stew pot to feed General Arnold and his
aides. As they ate, they talked, and I stood back ready
to serve, and listened. They talked about routes and
marching orders and other military things I didn't understand. Twice they mentioned William Heron in a
friendly way. I thought that was strange; but I didn't
worry about it much, because I couldn't get it out of
my mind that right at that moment Sam might be in
Redding somewhere. But what was I going to do about
it? Of course he didn't know that Father was gone, and
it worried me that he might be afraid to come home.
Then there was the other side of it, which was that the
chances were that Sam wasn't in General Arnold's

troops anymore and probably was a hundred miles from Redding anyway. I knew I was being foolish; but I couldn't help myself, and after a bit I said, "Mother, I'd better go out and see to the livestock."

"All right," she said. "But don't be long, I may need you to help with the gentlemen here."

I went through the kitchen out to the barnyard, and then around to the front. It was full dark and the rain was spitting against me, soaking my face. Across the road some troops stood in the church doorway smoking pipes. I crossed over. A soldier barred my way. "I'm looking for Sam Meeker," I said. "Is he here?"

"Who are you?"

"I'm his brother," I said.

"You better get an order from an officer."

My heart jumped. "Is Sam here?"

"Better go find an officer," he insisted.

Another soldier turned to us. "Don't make such a fuss," he said. "Let him go."

"This is Tory country, I don't trust any of them."

"Oh come on, the boy's not lying. Sam's from around here somewhere, I know that."

"Go get him yourself then," the first soldier said. "I don't want any part of it."

"Wait here," the other one said, "I'll see if I can find Sam." He went in, leaving the church door open. I could see soldiers sprawled out in the pews and lying in the aisles, trying to sleep. Some of them were drink-

ing from canteens, or chewing on hard loaves of bread.
The ones who wanted to smoke had come to the door
because it wasn't right to smoke in a church. They were
a ragged-looking lot of men, their clothing dirty and
torn and most of them not even having proper uniforms. They needed shaves and their hair was wild and
uncombed.

I saw the soldier work his way through the crowd,
looking around. I saw him bend down and touch somebody. And then Sam was coming up the aisle toward me.
He looked older and raggedy too, and he hadn't
shaved, either. He got to the door. For a moment we
stared at each other. And then he put his arms around
me and hugged me, and I hugged him back. "Timmy,"
he said. I couldn't say anything. It felt so good to hug
him I began to cry. Then he began to cry, too, and we
stood there in the church door hugging each other and
crying all over ourselves. After a couple of minutes we
started feeling foolish crying that way in front of the
soldiers, and we stopped hugging.

"I wanted to come over to see you," he said, "but I
didn't know if you all hated me."

"Hated you?"

"I thought you might."

"Sam, Father's—"

"I know," he said. "That's why I thought you might
not want to see me. I didn't know what to do."

"How did you find out about Father?" I asked.

"The commissary officers found out that I know about dealing in cattle. I've been working with them a lot, looking for beef. And I met somebody from Salem who'd heard about what happened to Father. I think he got it from the Platts." He touched my shoulder. "How's Mother?"

"She's not mad at you either. None of us are."

"Let's go over," he said. "I haven't been home for two years. Who's in the tavern?"

"The generals."

"Then I'll have to stay in the barn. I'm not supposed to leave my company. Wait, I'll tell somebody where I'm going just in case they want me."

He went into the church. In a moment he was back, and we ducked across the road through the rain and around behind the house to the barn.

I lit a lantern. "You've changed, Tim."

"I'm more of a grownup, now."

"I can see that. Has it been hard on you and Mother?"

"We even have to work on Sundays," I said. "Sam, what have they done with Father?"

He sucked in a mouthful of air. "I don't know. Put him in prison, probably."

"But why? He wasn't doing anything, he wasn't a real Tory, he was just against the war."

"He was selling beef to the British."

"No he wasn't, he was selling beef to Mr. Bogardus. He didn't care who bought it."

"What difference does it make? It was getting to the British. It comes down to the same thing. He was selling beef to the enemy."

"Are you against Father, Sam?"

"No, but Father's against me."

"You ran away," I said

"He told me to leave. I didn't want to fight with him, but he threw me out."

"He cried when you left," I said.

"I know. You told me that before. Don't think I was happy about leaving. I felt terrible. I remember running down that road in the rain being mad and cursing him for what he did. But all the while I was cursing I kept remembering things like our trips over to Verplancks Point, and him taking me down to New Haven to get admitted to Yale, and buying me new clothes there, and everything else, and finally I stopped cursing and I just felt terrible and wished we hadn't fought. But it was too late. That's two years ago, Tim."

"Don't you feel bad about Father being in prison, Sam?"

"Yes." He didn't say anything for a minute. "As a matter of fact I thought I might be able to get him out. I even went to see General Arnold about it. But I couldn't even find out where he is. Nobody knows."

"Well maybe you can try again."

"Tim, I don't want to talk about it anymore, I'm too tired."

He was tired all right. "Can't you write somebody a letter?"

"Tim, I don't want to argue about it anymore."

"I'll stop arguing if you promise to try to get Father out."

"I can't get him out. I tried."

"But you can try again," I said.

"For God's sake, Tim."

I shut up. I didn't want to spoil it by having a fight. We stared at each other for a minute. Then he said, "Can you get me something to eat?"

"I'll tell Mother you're here."

I slipped across the barnyard, through the kitchen and into the tavern. The generals and their aides had finished eating, and were drinking rum and water, and talking over plans. Mother gave me a cross look. "Where have you been?"

"There's something wrong with Old Pru's leg. I think you better come out and look at it."

"It'll have to wait," she said.

"I think you ought to look at it now, Mother."

It wasn't like me to insist on anything that way and she got the idea. "All right, just a moment," she said. "See if the gentlemen need more rum." I filled the glasses and helped her clear the plates, and then we went out through the kitchen into the barnyard. "What's happened, Tim?"

"Sam's in the barn."

She stopped dead. "Sam's here?"

"That's where I've been—looking for him. I thought he might be here with General Arnold."

She started to run, but then she thought better of it and walked steadily out there. When Sam saw her he came a little way out of the barn shadows. For a moment he and Mother stared at each other, and then they began to hug, and I came up and put my arms around both of them and hugged them together. Then Mother pushed back and stared at him. "I haven't seen you for two years, Sam," she said.

He grinned. "Do I look different?"

"Dirtier," she said.

He laughed. "Is that all?"

"No, older," she said. "You've gotten older."

"Tim has too. I hardly recognized him."

"He's had to grow up fast," Mother said. "He didn't have much choice."

"I thought you'd all be mad at me," he said. "I didn't know if you'd be speaking to me."

"Oh we're willing to speak to you all right," she said. "We need you back home."

"Hey, Tim, I thought you were going to bring me something to eat." He was trying to change the subject.

"I forgot," I said.

"Tim, get your brother some bread and a piece of that ham that's hanging in the kitchen."

I went back to the kitchen and got the food. I knew they were going to have an argument. When I got back to the barn Mother was saying, "Sam, we don't even know if he's alive. You have to come home now. We need you."

That was the first time I'd ever heard her admit that Father might be dead. Sam winced. It hurt him. "I don't think he's dead, Mother."

I handed him the food.

"Oh lovely," he said. "Thanks." He tore off a piece of the ham with his teeth and then stuffed a hunk of bread into his mouth.

I said, "Is that the way they eat in the army?" I knew it wasn't going to do any good to argue with Sam; he wasn't going to change his mind. I didn't want Mother to have a fight with him.

He swallowed. "I guess we figure if we're lucky enough to have anything to eat, we don't care how we eat it."

But Mother wouldn't give up. "Sam, you have to come home. We need you. Your people have taken Father from us; they'll have to give us you in return."

"Mother, I can't come home. That's desertion, they hang people for that."

"When is your enlistment up, Sam?"

He frowned. "In two months. But I'm going to re-enlist."

"No, Sam. You have to come home."

"Mother," I said, "don't argue with him. You can't make him change his mind."

"He's just being stubborn," she said.

"God, Mother," he said, "I came to pay a visit and first Tim badgered me about Father and now you're badgering me about coming home. I can't come home until it's over. It's my duty to stay and fight."

"You have a duty to your family, too."

"My duty to my country comes first. Now please everybody stop arguing with me."

"And get killed in the meantime," she said.

"Maybe," he said.

We were quiet for a moment. Then he said, "We've made a promise, a group of us, not to quit until the Redcoats are beaten. We've made a pledge to each other."

"Oh Sam, that's a foolish promise."

I said, "Mother, stop arguing with him."

"You're both fools," she said.

He was getting angry. "For God's sake, Mother, people are out there dying for you."

"Well they can stop dying," Mother said. "I don't need anybody's death."

"Let him alone, Mother," I said. "He isn't going to

change his mind."

We were silent, and I knew she was trying to accept it. "All right," she said finally. "All right."

We changed the subject. We talked about the crops, and about people, and he gave us a message to take to Betsy Read. "We'll probably be moving out soon," he said. "I don't know. Tell her I'll try to see her if I can." He paused for a minute. "I'd better go now before somebody misses me."

He hugged Mother and then he hugged me, and turned and slipped through the rain and the night out of the barnyard. We watched him go, knowing that we might never see him again. Then we went back into the tavern.

I had a funny feeling about seeing Sam. It wasn't just that he was more grown-up or that I was more grown-up. It was something else. For the first time in my life I knew that Sam was wrong about something; I knew that I understood something better than he did. Oh, I used to argue with him before, but that was mostly to show that I wasn't going to just agree with everything he said. But this time I *knew* he was wrong. He was staying in the army because he *wanted* to stay in the army, not because of duty or anything else. He liked the excitement of it. Oh, I guessed he was miserable a lot of the time when he was cold and hungry and maybe being shot at, but still, he was part of something big, he thought that what he was doing was important. It felt good to be part of it, and I knew that was the real reason why he didn't want to come home.

Knowing that about Sam gave me a funny feeling. I didn't feel like his little brother so much anymore, I felt more like his equal.

XII

IN JUNE OF THAT YEAR, 1777, WE FOUND OUT THAT
Father was dead. He'd been dead for a month. It had
happened pretty much as we'd guessed it: he'd been
sent to a prison ship in New York. There was one
funny thing about it, though—it wasn't a Rebel prison
ship, it was a British one. We never did figure out how
that had happened. It had just come out of the con-

fusion of the war somehow. It didn't much matter, in
the end, though. Those prison ships were terrible places
—filthy and baking hot in summer and freezing in
winter and of course nothing but slop to eat. The worst
part was disease: if anybody got sick with anything serious, everybody on the ship was liable to get it. That's
what had happend to Father: they'd had an epidemic of
cholera on the prison ship he'd been on. About forty or
fifty people had died from it, and he'd been one of
them. They'd buried him someplace on Long Island,
but we weren't sure where. Mother said, "After the
war we'll find where he lies and have a headstone made
for him." But I don't think even she believed we'd be
able to do that.

We found all this out from one of the men who'd
been taken away during the raid on Redding that
spring. He'd been put in the same ship, and he'd been
with Father when he died. "Before he died he asked
me to make sure you knew what had happened. He
said, 'Tell them that I love them, and say that I forgive Sam, he's a brave boy but he's headstrong.' The
last thing he said was, 'And now I go to enjoy the freedom war has brought me.' "

But Father wasn't the only one who died. Two days
after we found out about Father, Betsy Read came
down to the tavern. I gave her a pot of beer. "Did you
hear about Jeremiah Sanford?" she said.

"No," I said.

"He's dead," she said.

"Jerry? He's dead?"

"Nobody understands it. They put him on a prison ship and he got sick and died in three weeks. It doesn't make any sense. You can understand why they took Mr. Rogers or Captain Betts, but why imprison a ten-year-old boy?"

"What harm could he have done them? This war has turned men into animals," Mother said.

"They sunk his body in Long Island Sound in a weighted sack," Betsy said. "So his parents can't even get him back. I don't understand it, what did they want him for?"

"They're animals now, they're all beasts," Mother said.

"I think they are," Betsy said. "Sam should have come home."

It was the first time I'd ever heard her say anything against Sam and his ideals. "I told him that," I said. "He said he'd taken a pledge with some friends to stick it out until they won."

"Does he still think they're going to win?" Betsy said.

"Maybe they will," I said.

Betsy shook her head. "Even Father says things are bad for the Patriots."

I looked at her curiously. "Don't you want them to win?"

"I don't care who wins anymore. I just want it to be over."

"Sam wouldn't like you to talk like that."

"I don't care," she said. "When I see him I'm going to tell him. For three years they've been fighting and all we've had is death and hunger. Your father is dead, Jeremiah Sanford is dead, Sam Barlow is dead, David Fairchild is dead, Stephen Fairchild was wounded, and more."

My mother nodded. "Right at the beginning Life said it would be that way. He said, 'In war the dead pay the debts for the living.' But he didn't think he would have to pay himself."

So Father had forgiven Sam, and I think Mother did, although she never said so. But for myself I wasn't sure. I knew I'd be glad to see him, and have him at home: but still I felt it was partly his fault that Father had died. Oh, he hadn't captured Father or thrown him in prison or given him cholera or anything like that. But he was fighting on their side, and I couldn't easily forget about that. Yet of course it was a British prison ship he'd died on. It seemed to me that everybody was to blame, and I decided that I wasn't going to be on anybody's side any more: neither one of them was right.

So summer passed and it became winter once more and people were suffering worse than ever from want. Luckily, there wasn't any more fighting around Redding. Anyway, in the winter they didn't fight much. Nobody liked to fight in the cold, and when there was snow on the ground it was hard to march and easy to get sick. The Continental Army was encamped at a place called Valley Forge out in Pennsylvania somewhere. We didn't know whether Sam was there or not. From what we'd heard they were practically starving and hadn't any clothes. I was just as glad; it made me hope that the Rebels were at the end of their rope and would have to give up pretty soon and end this terrible war. I didn't even mind that Sam might be suffering with cold and hunger. It would serve him right; we were pretty hungry ourselves.

Sam began writing us letters every once in a while— every two or three months especially after he heard that Father was dead. He didn't tell us where he was in his letters. Mostly they'd be about places he'd been. Sometimes Betsy Read would get a letter from him, too, and she'd come down to tell us about it. So time passed. The year 1777 ended and 1778 began. Spring came, then summer and fall, and we harvested. Oh how I hated the war. All of life was like running on a treadmill. I was fourteen, I should have been going to school all this while and learning something. Maybe by this time I would have begun to think about going to New Haven to study at Yale. I wasn't much interested in Latin or Greek, but in the last couple of years I'd learned a lot about buying and selling and the tavern business, and I wanted to study calculating and surveying and the agricultural sciences: I thought I might have a career in business. I might apprentice myself to a merchant in New Haven or New York, or even London, to learn the art of trade. Sam owed it to me to come home and help Mother run the tavern for a couple of years while I started to make my way in the world.

But until the war ended there was nothing for me to do but tread water. Prices kept on spiraling upward, merchandise grew shorter and shorter in supply, and everybody seemed to be in debt. You couldn't refuse a hungry widow who'd lost her husband in the war some cloth or molasses on credit, but then how could we pay for new merchandise ourselves?

We couldn't get over to Verplancks Point that fall. The Rebels were holding all of northern Westchester County—Peekskill, Verplancks, Crompond, all of it. There was no way for us to get any cattle through. There wasn't much cattle around, anyway. Bit by bit people had been slaughtering their stock for food. However, Mother and I had been able to get hold of eight scrawny cows, mainly from people who owed us a lot of money. There wasn't much to them, but with food in such short supply I figured we could get a pretty good price for them if we could get them to a British commissary somewhere. Not that I cared which side we sold them to, but the British were the ones who had money—they had the whole English exchequer behind them. The Continentals were paying off in commissary scrip, which would be totally worthless if they lost. I'd heard that there was a British commissary in White Plains, which was about twenty-five miles southwest across the New York State line. I figured I might be able to drive the cattle down there through the woods. It would be very risky, but better than going hungry. And we needed some money to buy goods to keep the tavern and the store going. If the business died, we'd really be out of luck.

Hunger is a pretty terrible thing. It's like going around all day with a nail in your shoe. You try to put it out of your mind, but you never really quite forget it, and when something reminds you of it, like reading about a big meal in a story or seeing a stack of bread, it really hurts—I mean it just plain hurts. It makes you feel weak, and you get sick easily, too. That winter everybody had colds and went around sniffling most of the time. Some people got really sick, and then their families would have to scrape up extra food to feed them with. Oh, I don't mean that people were dying from hunger. Nobody was actually starving to death, but most were hungry a lot of the time.

All through November I tried to find out about the British commissary—whether it really existed or not, and where it actually was. But I couldn't find out anything I really trusted. It was all rumors—the commissary was at White Plains. No, it wasn't at White Plains, it was at Horseneck. Yes, it was at White Plains after all, but the Rebels had it under seige. And so forth. I didn't want to go until I was sure: if I ran into Rebels I'd lose the cattle and probably be put in prison myself. It was only worth the risk if I were sure where the commissary was: otherwise we might just as well eat the cattle ourselves.

So that was the situation on December 3, 1778, when Sam came back to Redding. That morning he walked into the tavern. He looked thin and tired. There were black circles under his eyes and his uniform was torn in about six places. He'd lost his belt and was wearing a piece of rope around his waist, and his hat wasn't an army hat but just an ordinary fur cap. But he was glad to be home, and grinning. "Hello, everybody," he said.

Mother was out in the kitchen and I'd been stoking up the fire. "Sam," I shouted. "Mother, Sam's here."

She burst into the tavern and began to hug him, and I hugged him, too, and then he crouched down in front of the fire and ate a bowl of porridge with honey that

Mother brought him. "This is the first time I've been warm for a week," he said.

So we asked him all the natural questions: where he'd been and where he was going and so forth. "I'm going to be in Redding for a while," he said. "General Putnam is bringing a couple of regiments here for winter encampment. We're going up to Lonetown and hole up until spring."

"What's the idea of that?"

"The rumor is that we're supposed to be situated to move either west to the Hudson or south to Long Island Sound in case of a British attack either place. Some say we're mainly here to watch over the magazines at Middletown. I don't know—those are the rumors. But we're building huts so I guess we'll be here for awhile."

"How did you get off?"

"I've had a bit of luck. Colonel Parsons—Samuel Holden Parsons, that is—has moved into the Betts' house. An adjutant came around and asked if any of us were from this area and I said I was, and Colonel Parsons brought me into town this morning to show him around." Sam grinned. "To the ladies, mostly. I told him that there weren't any ladies in Redding except my mother and my girl. He said they would do, so Mother you'd better put on your best dress."

Mother smiled, but I don't think she thought it was

very funny. "You're so thin, Sam," she said. "Are the troops all starving?"

"Everybody in the country is hungry," he said. "It's going to be worse this winter, too. Have you got any cattle, Tim?"

I was proud that he asked me instead of Mother. "Eight," I said. "They're not much to look at."

"Butcher them and hide the meat. Or sell it. You can get a good price for the hides from the troops. Sell what you can. I promise you, the stock will be stolen."

Mother frowned. "You mean your troops are stealing from your own people?"

"A starving man will steal food from babies." He shook his head. "There's a lot you don't understand. All of us have seen good friends killed. I had a friend bayoneted, and it took him six hours to die, screaming all the while. All we could do was hold his hand and wait. I saw a captain I loved blown in half by a cannon ball. He was the best officer we ever had, he worried about his men, he put them first. He never ate before we were fed, and I've seen him go without to give his portion to a sick man. The redcoats blew him in half, right into two pieces with his guts dangling out of both parts." He shivered. "After a few things like that you don't give a damn for anybody but your friends anymore. You kill Redcoats the way you butcher pigs. The troops know that Redding is a Tory town. As far as they're concerned taking cattle from Tories is getting revenge. Sure, lots of them would steal from anybody, whether they were Tories or Patriots or anything else. Some are unscrupulous when they're hungry and some are unscrupulous by nature and they'll take whatever they think they can get away with. Of course the majority of men are honest and won't steal, but if they decide you're Tories, they'll have no compunction about taking your beef. And let me tell you, it's pretty easy to decide somebody's a Tory when you haven't eaten anything but hard tack and pork fat for weeks. I've done it myself."

"Sam."

"I won't apologize."

"War turns men into animals," Mother said.

"I was ashamed of it afterwards," Sam said, "but not very and my belly was full." He nodded slowly. "Tim, butcher the cattle. Let the meat freeze and hide it in the loft under the hay until you need it." He glanced out the window toward the Betts' house. "I better go. Colonel Parsons may be waiting for me."

"Don't go yet, Sam," Mother said. "We've just seen you."

"I'll be around all winter, Mother. Maybe I can get attached to Colonel Parson's staff. I'll try to get a pass if I can. Anyway, I can always slip out at night. It's risky. Colonel Parson's is not harsh, but General Putnam is in charge. He's a great patriot, but he's rough and tough on men who shirk their duty. A hundred lashes for desertion and if there's too much of it, I know he'll hang some people as an example. That's the kind of man he is. But I'll be back to visit again one way or another."

He left. We walked out into the yard with him, and he crossed over to the Betts' house and went in. "He's so thin," Mother said. "I worry that he'll get sick. I couldn't bear to lose another, Tim." All at once she began to sob. It only lasted ten seconds. Then she turned and went into the house, and when I went in a minute later she was calmly scrubbing some beets.

After December 3rd we began to get used to the sight of soldiers constantly around town. There were always messengers going by and trains of supply wagons crunching over the snow and sometimes groups of soldiers on work parties would appear at the tavern for beer. Having the troops around was good for business. Some of the officers lodged in houses around about. Often in the evening they came up to the tavern to play cards and drink or smoke. Business was good—or rather it would have been good if we had had anything to sell, and people had had anything to pay for it with besides commissary scrip.

The biggest demand was for liquor. Life at the encampment was cold and miserable and the only relief for them was drinking. They didn't care what it was—rum, whiskey, cider, anything we could get. Whiskey was pretty hard to get. The General Assembly had made it illegal to distill whiskey because it was made from grain, and grain was needed for food. Rum was easier to get and we could usually get cider, because every farmer made it. I spent a lot of time riding around among the farmers buying whatever they had. They'd often have rum they'd taken in trade for livestock. I could offer them good prices for liquor because we could get good prices for it: the officers didn't care how much they paid for liquor. As they said when they were drinking, "A short life but a merry one." Which of them knew when he was going to die?

Of course the ordinary soldiers didn't have much fun. For one thing, there was always the snow. It came down in a great blizzard about a week after the troops had started to build the encampment. Their huts were not finished and they were forced to work in bitter cold and storm. The cold was a problem. The huts were really just tiny log cabins with big stone fireplaces making the whole rear wall. In cold weather they had a lot of trouble getting the mortar to set. Because of this the chimneys leaked so badly that half the smoke blew back into the room. The snow made hewing wood difficult, too. Sam told us that they were having an awful time getting the huts finished. Even when they were done they weren't much to live in—twelve soldiers jammed into a 14 by 16 room, breathing more smoke than air and having to stumble over people whenever they wanted to move around. And the snow never stopped falling. By January it covered the countryside three feet deep, so that the stone walls disappeared. You could drive a sled over the snow anywhere you wanted without paying attention to where the roads were.

Sam was able to get into town every week or ten days. Colonel Parsons used him as a messenger a lot because he knew his way around Redding. Sometimes he would come in with a commissary officer looking for lime or nails or leather or all the hundreds of things armies need. The idea was that Sam might know who had things. Often he'd come into the tavern and ask me if I knew who had hay or sleds or something else to sell.

To be honest, I felt uneasy about telling him such things. The commissary people always paid for whatever they bought, but it was usually in scrip, and on top of it, the farmer didn't have much choice about selling or not. But I couldn't bring myself to lie to Sam. It was something I'd never done.

All the time Sam was after us to butcher the cattle. I didn't know what to do. The idea of selling them to the British was gone. With all the Rebel troops around it was too risky trying to move cattle anywhere. Besides, it would have been next to impossible in that deep snow. Still, I kept hoping that I could find someone who'd offer me a good deal for them. But Sam was pressing me. "I'm warning you, Tim, sooner or later somebody's going to get them."

"I thought General Putnam gave strict orders against stealing."

"Oh he did, and knowing General Putnam he'll hang any soldier he catches stealing. He's tough as nails but he's honest. Besides, he wants the people to come around to our side, and if he lets the troops forage, he'll lose all sympathy with the populace. Oh, I know him. He's had a lot of men flogged already for disobeying orders, and I'm sure he's just itching to catch somebody stealing so he can make an example of him."

"Then what's the worry?"

"Don't be stupid, Tim. A lot of men will take a chance anyway, especially when they're drunk. You wait; sooner or later they'll get into your beef if you don't watch it."

Mother and I kept churning it around between us. She figured Sam was right. "You know what happened to Sally Myles' heifer." Mrs. Myles was a widow who lived alone in a tiny hovel in Redding. She had a few tough chickens and one scrawny cow. She kept going mostly by selling milk and eggs to the people around.

A few days earlier a half dozen drunken soldiers had noticed her cow in her barn, butchered it right there, and carried the slabs of beef back to the encampment in the dark.

"I know," I said. "But the thing we need most is rum and the only way to pay for it is with cattle."

That was the beginning of January. We decided to stick it out through the month. There was a rumor going around that the British were forming up in New York City and were going to raid towns on Long Island. What that meant nobody knew, but some believed that the men from the encampment would be called down there to fight. I just couldn't make up my mind.

The weeks went by. There was nothing anybody wanted but to get through this terrible winter. It didn't seem that the war could really go on much longer. Even Sam thought it would have to end soon. We talked about it one evening when he was there for a short visit. We were sitting in front of the taproom fire one night in late January. "I think something decisive will happen in the spring," he said. "The English government realizes by now that they're not going to beat us easily."

"Maybe they figured you're too starved and tired to fight much longer."

He shook his head seriously. "They might be right,"

he said. "The other day some of the men were actually talking mutiny. A lot of them have no blankets, they're short of food, and the pay hasn't come through. A bunch of them decided to march to Hartford and demand their pay. They were about to start out when General Putnam rode up and talked them out of it. Then he had a couple of the ringleaders shot right there. He shows no mercy when he thinks he's right."

Suddenly he stopped talking. "What was that?" I'd heard it, too—a kind of a thump and then a cow bawling. We listened. There were noises coming from outside somewhere.

"Sounds like something's bothering the cattle," I said.

"There are people out there," Sam shouted. "Let's go."

We ran out through the kitchen toward the barn. It was dark, but there was nearly a full moon reflected on the snow and plenty enough light to see what had happened. The barn doors were open. Two cows were standing in front of the barn blinking, and we could see two more behind. We dashed into the barn. Four of the cows were gone. "Jesus damn," I shouted.

"Pen 'em up," Sam shouted. "They'll be butchering the others somewhere near. There's no chance of driving them very far in this snow."

He darted around the house toward the road, his

eyes following the hoof prints in the snow. I snatched up a shovel and drove the remaining four cattle back into the barn with the handle. They were balky, and it took me a few minutes to get them inside and the door shut and latched. Then I raced across the snow around the house to the road. There I stopped and swung my eyes across the horizon. I saw nothing, but distantly I heard the noise of shouting, off toward the far end of the training ground. I ran in the direction of the sounds, and then suddenly I saw three men walking toward me through the moonlight, side by side. I stopped and waited. They came up. The one in the middle was Sam. His nose was bleeding and there was a cut in his chin. His hands were tied behind his back.

I stood in the open white snow field, surrounded by shadowy trees. "Sam," I shouted.

"Timmy, get Colonel Parsons," he cried. "They're taking me in as a cattle thief." I went cold. Then I turned and ran.

XIII

"I WANT TO SEE COLONEL PARSONS, PLEASE, SIR," I SAID.

The adjutant stared at me through the half-opened door. "What about?"

"Sam Meeker sent me. He's been arrested as a cattle thief."

"Colonel Parsons can't be troubled about that."

"But it's all a mistake," I said. "He didn't do it, he was chasing the ones who did."

The adjutant laughed. "Sure," he said. "He didn't steal the cows, they followed him out of the barn of their own accord."

"Please," I begged. "It's true. We were sitting there—"

"Enough," he said. "Colonel Parsons is in bed. Come back in the morning and perhaps he'll see you then."

There wasn't any point in arguing with him, I realized. I would have to see Colonel Parsons in the morning. The cows were still loose, and I had to do something about them, anyway. "Thank you, sir," I said and turned and ran back over the empty spaces of snow toward the training ground. In the brightness of the moonlight it was easy to see the forms of three cattle standing in the middle of the snowy field. As fast as I could I pushed out into the snow toward them. As I came up I saw the fourth cow lying on the ground. It was dead, half-buried in the snow and its belly had been sliced open, its guts glistening wet in the moonlight.

The three living cows were staggering around in the deep snow and bawling unhappily. I found a stick in the treeline at the edge of the field and began driving the cattle home. It was a terrible job. They hated floundering around in the deep snow and balked constantly. It took me over half an hour to get them safely back into the barn. I threw them down some hay and then I went into the tavern.

Mother was sitting in front of the fire, looking worried. "I saw you coming across the road," she said. "Where's Sam?"

"They arrested him," I said. "The ones who stole the cattle beat him up, and then they said he'd stolen the cattle himself and marched him off somewhere."

"Back to the encampment?"

"I guess so," I said. "They'll let him go in the morning, won't they? I mean all we have to do is explain it, don't we?"

She shook her head. "I have a terrible foreboding, Timothy. I want to pray."

"The dead cow is still out there, Mother. I want to get it before somebody else does."

"If we haven't got time to pray to the Lord for help, we haven't got much time at all, have we?" So we got down on our knees and prayed for Sam. Then I got the butchering knives out and we went together into the snow field and cut up the cow. The meat was already beginning to freeze, making it hard to cut. We had to chop it into small pieces, too, because neither of us was strong enough to carry off a whole side of beef by ourselves. It took us an hour of struggling to cut the animal up and carry it home. We hid it in the barn loft under the hay; it would keep well enough in that cold weather.

In the morning I went back to Captain Betts' house to talk to Colonel Parsons. They made me wait around outside the door for half an hour before they let me in. Colonel Parsons seemed nice enough but awfully busy. I told him the story, but he shrugged. "It surprises me that Sam would be taken for a thief. I thought he was a man of greater patriotism than that, but people fool you."

"He didn't do it, sir. These other men——"

He held his hand up to stop me. "I know, you told me that. In any case there isn't anything I can do. They've taken him out to the encampment, and it'll be up to General Putnam to do what he wants. I'd get out there in a hurry, though. The General is determined to make an example of somebody. It could go hard with Sam. General Putnam is a great and dedicated patriot and he does not take defection from duty lightly."

Now I was beginning to get worried. At first it had seemed that it wouldn't take much to straighten the mistake out. After all, it was our cows that had been stolen. Surely they'd believe us when we told them Sam hadn't taken them. But the way Colonel Parsons talked about it bothered me. He didn't seem to care very much whether Sam was guilty or not. It didn't seem very important to him. I said so to Mother.

She looked sad. "They've seen so much death, these soldiers. What does the life of one more man mean to them?" She sighed. "Now we must go down to the encampment and try to save him."

We couldn't both go. One of us had to stay and watch the tavern. We were required by law to keep open most of the time in case travelers came by. In any case, it was risky to leave the place unguarded. We decided that Mother ought to go. She was an adult, her word would go better with General Putnam than mine would. She put on her bonnet and wrapped a shawl around her shoulders, and started out. I stood in the yard and watched her go down the road until she was merely a black spot in the field of white. Then I went out to the barn to look the cattle over more carefully, in case any of them had been hurt. Not that it mattered much; I was determined to butcher them as soon as I had a chance.

Betsy Read came into the tavern a half hour later. She hadn't bothered to comb her hair properly and she looked scared. "What's happened to Sam? I heard he was arrested for something."

"For stealing our own cattle," I said.

She got angry. "Sam didn't do that," she said.

"I didn't say he did." I told her the story. "Mother's really worried. I've never seen her so down, not even when we found out Father was dead. She bore up when he got captured and bore up when we learned he'd died, but she isn't bearing up now. She's trying, but she isn't bearing up."

"It's not having enough to eat," Betsy said. "You don't have the strength to keep your spirits up." She sat and dropped her head on the taproom table. "What are we going to do about Sam?"

"I don't know. Mother's finding out."

"Will they hang him if they think he did it?"

"I don't know," I said. It seemed a good chance that they would the way everybody was talking about how hard General Putnam was, but I didn't want to think about that. "Probably they would just put him in prison."

"I wouldn't mind that," Betsy said. "At least he wouldn't be able to get himself into anymore trouble."

I didn't say anything. All I could think about was Father and Jerry Sanford. "Could your father do anything?"

"Maybe," she said. "I'll talk to him right away."

She left. I was glad; I didn't want to dwell on Sam. There were plenty of things to do to keep myself busy. Besides my regular chores I had to start getting ready to butcher. This meant putting up hooks for hanging the meat in the barn. We'd never butchered eight head of cattle at one time, and we didn't have the hanging space for them. To occupy my mind I spent my spare moments figuring out the best way to do it.

And of course people kept coming in. There were the usual customers—officers wanting food, ordinary soldiers wanting a chance to get warm, Redding people buying things. There were also people asking about Sam. Word had got around, and people wanted to know what had happened. Mr. Beach came in and Mr. Heron and Captain Betts.

I expected that Mother would be back by noon but she wasn't, and by mid-afternoon I began to worry. I kept looking out the window about every five minutes, but still she didn't come. I got the supper stew started— it was about all we served to anybody anymore. It began to get dark, and then she came in. She looked exhausted. She slumped down in a chair by the fire. I gave her a glass of rum to warm her up, and was about to ask her what had happened, but just then some officers came in wanting dinner and some drinks and we got busy. It wasn't until an hour later when we'd got the officers settled over their rum and water that she could tell me the story out in the kitchen.

She'd had to wait until the middle of the afternoon to see General Putnam. The aides kept putting her off and sending her away, but she stuck it out and finally she got to see him. He was curt; he really didn't want to take the time. She told the story. He merely shrugged. "You see what the problem is, Tim. Those two men who brought him in have sworn it was Sam who stole the animals." Her voice was slow and tired and hopeless. "Sam wasn't supposed to be here; he was supposed to be on duty with Colonel Parsons at the Betts' house."

"But Colonel Parsons didn't care, he always let Sam come over and visit."

"Still, he wasn't supposed to. Officially Sam had deserted his post. Why should they believe Sam about the cattle over the other men? Why should they believe me? I'm his mother, I'd certainly lie to save him." She paused. "Go out and see if the officers need anything. And bring me some more rum. I'm cold."

They wouldn't let us see Sam, but a few days later Colonel Read came into the tavern and sat down with Mother and me. He looked serious. "I've been down to the encampment," he said. "I've talked with some of the officers there. I'm afraid it looks bad for Sam."

"Would you like some rum, Colonel Read?" Mother asked. Her voice was harsh. "I'm going to have some myself." Without waiting for him to answer she brought the rum and poured two glasses.

"Thank you," Colonel Read said.

"Why is it bad for Sam, sir?" I asked.

He sipped at the rum. "Here's the problem. Those soldiers Sam caught with the cattle are scared to death Putnam will simply decide to hang them all as an example. They're prepared to tell any kind of lie about Sam to get themselves off. If it were just Sam's word against somebody else's, it might be different, but there are two of them, and if they tell the same story, they can be convincing." He shook his head. "Then there's the fact that Sam comes from a Tory family."

"We're not really Tories, though," I said. "Father wasn't, none of us are."

"That's not the way General Putnam's going to see it."

"But won't there be a trial, sir?" I said.

"Oh yes," Colonel Read said. "A regular court-martial. There'll be a presiding justice and a board of officers acting as the jury. But we have to face the fact that the board will do whatever they think General Putnam wants. And if they decide that Putnam wants to make an example of somebody, they'll hang—they'll bend over backwards to satisfy him, regardless of the evidence."

"What can we do?"

"Pray," Colonel Read said. "Actually there are some others going to be tried at the same time. A butcher named Edward Jones from Ridgefield who was caught spying for the British, another man for stealing shoes and another for desertion, I think. So there's always hope that they'll get enough blood out of the others to let Sam go. His war record is good and that'll help."

The trial was set for February 6th, three weeks away. There was nothing to do but wait it out. I didn't know what to think. I didn't see how they could find Sam guilty—he'd fought for three years, he'd risked his life, how could they decide to punish him for something he hadn't done? It just didn't make sense.

Two or three times I went out to the encampment to

try to see him, but they wouldn't let me. They had him locked up in a cabin they were using for a prison, but they wouldn't even tell me which one it was, because they were afraid I'd smuggle a weapon to him or help him escape or something. After I'd been out there a couple of times they realized who I was, so they wouldn't even let me into the encampment. I figured I could sneak in after dark if I had to. They'd cut down most of the trees around about for lumber and fire-wood, but there were rocks on the sides of the steep hill which let down into the encampment, and I figured I could come down in their shadows. But there wasn't any use in trying until I knew where they'd hidden him, so I gave up for the moment and waited.

I was beginning to get worried about Mother. She'd never been one for drinking much—just a glass of rum punch occasionally when she was chilled or sick. But she'd begun to take it more. Not that she was drunk all the time or anything like that. But sometimes I'd come upon her standing by herself with her eyes empty and staring and a little glass of rum in her hands. She'd hardly notice I was there until I spoke to her. It wasn't much as I say, but she was changed, and it bothered me.

Finally February 6th came. Colonel Read came in first thing in the morning. "I'm going out to the encampment," he said. "I'll bring back news tonight."

All day long I was so nervous I couldn't eat, I couldn't sit still. I had to keep moving around and I was glad when people came in wanting food or hot drinks so I could keep busy. Once two officers came in and ordered hot rum to warm up with. One of them said, "Did you see any of the court-martial?"

"No," the other said. "Why bother, Putnam's determined to hang 'em all anyway."

I shuddered, but I said nothing.

It was after dark when Colonel Read came in. He was tired; his shoulders were sagging and his face was grim. He didn't have to say anything at all: I knew what had happened.

"Where's your mother?"

"She's out back in the kitchen."

I went and got her. She stood in the doorway, saying nothing. "Mrs. Meeker, I have bad news. They're going to execute Sam."

She smiled politely. "That isn't news, Colonel Read. I've known that for three weeks."

That was the story. The man who had been caught stealing shoes would get a hundred lashes. The deserter would get a hundred lashes. The butcher, Edward Jones, was to be hung. Sam Meeker, cattle thief, was to be shot. The executions would take place on a hill near the encampment on February 16th, a Tuesday. The Sunday before there would be a compulsory church attendance.

It surprised me that I didn't cry or faint or anything like that. I was numb and nervous and nothing more.

And I began making plans. The first thing I did was to go to see Colonel Parsons. He put me off twice because he knew what I was coming for, but as he was quartered next door to us he knew he'd have to see me sooner or later, and finally he did.

"I can't help you," he said bluntly. "The court-martial has decided and that's the end of it."

"Then who can help me, sir," I demanded.

He stared at me. "General Putnam. Nobody but General Putam."

"All right then, give me a note to him, sir."

"Why should I do that?" he asked.

"Because Sam didn't do it. You know that's true."

He stared at me. "Sir."

"Sir."

He put his head down in his hands. "War is hard, boy. Sometimes we do a lot of things we don't want to do. A lot of very good men have been killed in this war, and all we can do is hope that it's been worth it. Maybe it hasn't. Maybe in the end we'll conclude that. But I don't think so, I think it will be worth it, despite the death and destruction." He raised his head again and looked at me. "No," he said, "I don't think that Sam stole those cows. But I can't prove it and neither can you. Who knows, maybe he did do it after all? Maybe he had some kind of arrangement with those other men so as to throw suspicion off himself."

"Sam would never have done that."

He smacked his hand down on the desk. "Watch how you address me," he snapped.

I blushed. "I'm sorry, sir."

He put his hands behind his head and leaned back. "Do you want to know what General Putnam is thinking? It's this. He's thinking that he can't win the war if he doesn't keep the people on his side. He's thinking that he can't keep the people on his side if the troops are running amok among the civilian population—raping the women, stealing cattle, burning houses. He is determined to scare the wits out of the troops to keep them in line. And he's thinking that it doesn't matter very much who he executes to do it. So many men have died, so many mothers have wept, so many brothers and sisters have cried. He is thinking that in the long run if he executes somebody, he'll shorten the war and save more lives. It doesn't matter to him very much who he executes; one man's agony is like another's, one mother's tears are no wetter than anybody else's. And that's why he's going to have Sam shot."

"But Sam isn't guilty, sir."

"The court-martial says he was."

"But they're wrong."

He sat silent. I waited. Then he said, "Because I happen to believe you, I'm going to give you a letter to see General Putnam. But I am warning you right now that it won't do a bit of good. The one thing Putnam cannot do at this point is show clemency. If

[194]

he is going to make his point with the troops, he can't start letting people off easily."

He took up a piece of paper, wrote something on it swiftly, folded it and sealed it, and addressed it to General Putnam. Then he gave it to me and I left, running.

I ran most of the way out to the encampment over the packed snow. The sky was cloudy; there would be snow and more snow. I arrived at the gate, my breath rasping in my throat so hard I couldn't speak. I handed my letter to the guard. He took it and he called over a soldier. "Take this boy to General Putnam," he said.

We walked up the encampment street past a long line of huts. They were identical, a hundred of them with plumes of bluish smoke rising like a forest into the air. Soldiers were everywhere, cutting wood, cleaning things, drilling. Then we came to a house, bigger than the huts, but made of the same kind of logs. The soldier handed my letter to the guard at the door. The guard took it inside and in about five minutes he came back. "Just wait," he said.

I waited for half an hour and then an hour and then two hours. Officers went in and out, and still I waited. I got hungry but I didn't dare leave to go in search of something to eat. It became one in the afternoon, and then a soldier came out and brought me in.

General Putnam was sitting behind a rough trestle

table they'd set up for his desk. There were papers neatly arranged and ink bottles, pens, sand for blotting the ink, and a stack of maps. He was a big man of about sixty, with lots of white hair. He wore the Continental uniform of buff and blue. He did not look kind.

"Meeker?"

"Yes, sir."

"All right, let's have it."

He scared me. His voice was hard and his eyes flashed. But I told him the story exactly as it had happened and I finished by saying, "Sam wouldn't steal our own cattle. He just wouldn't. He's been fighting for three years, he's been a good soldier. And he didn't do it, sir, I swear it. I know because—"

"Enough," he said. "My time's valuable." He took up a piece of paper and quickly wrote something on it. Then he said, "I'll consider it. That'll be all."

"Sir, can I see my brother?"

He frowned at me. Then he shouted, "Sergeant, take this boy up to the stockade to see Sam Meeker. See that they stay six feet apart and pass nothing between them."

"Thank you, sir," I said, and then I followed the guard out.

The stockade was situated just at the bottom of the slope which dropped down into the encampment. It was a wooden hut like the others, but surrounded on all

sides by a picket fence to give the prisoners a place out-
doors to walk around in. Guards were posted at every
corner. There were some small holes cut in the fence,
each about a foot square. The guard put his face to one
of the holes and shouted, "Meeker, you've got a visitor
here." Then he drew a line in the snow with his toe
about six feet from the fence. "Stay behind that line,"
he said.

Sam's face appeared at the hole. He was dirty and
unshaven and his hair was uncombed. "Timmy," he
said.

"How are you, Sam?" I said.

"Oh I'm all right for a man about to die."

"Don't give up hope," I said. "I've just seen General
Putnam. He said he'd consider your case."

"Is that right?" he said. "Really?"

"He said he would."

"What did he actually say?" Sam said. "Does he
believe I'm not guilty?"

"I don't know," I said. "He didn't say."

"You're a good boy, Tim."

"Sam, how come they found you guilty?"

"I guess I didn't score enough telling points," he
said.

"No, really."

"The other men lied. They knew they were in for
it right from the moment I spotted them in the training
ground. I only saw one of them at first, and I levelled

the musket at him. But the other one was down on the ground in the shadows, gutting the cow, and he came up behind me and stuck his knife point against my back. So they got me. Then they bashed me around a little and took me in. Oh, they were smart. They had a story all worked out about hearing somebody shout 'Stop thief,' and seeing me driving the cattle across the training ground, and coming out to get me. And of course I wasn't supposed to be at home, anyway. I was supposed to be on duty at the Betts' house. So that went against me. And that was that."

"What else can we do, Sam?"

"Pray, I guess. You'd better have Mother do that; the Lord is more likely to believe her than you, Tim." He grinned. I grinned back; but I felt all sick inside.

Then the guard said, "Time's up, lad."

"I'll try to get back to see you again, Sam," I said.

"Say hello to Betsy for me," he said.

"Yes."

"And Mother," he said.

"Yes," I said. "And I'll try to think up some more telling points for General Putnam, too."

He grinned. "You're the best brother I've got, Tim."

I tried to grin back. "I better be."

"Come on you," the guard said. So I waved goodbye, and left.

THERE WAS NOTHING TO DO NOW BUT WAIT TO SEE
what General Putnam decided. So we waited. Betsy Read
came down to the tavern a lot, and we talked over a
lot of plans—escape plans and all that kind of thing.
But none of them seemed very good. A week passed.
And on Saturday, February 13th, Colonel Read came
up from the encampment with the word that General
Putnam had refused our plea for clemency.

I began to cry. "It's just so unfair, he fought for them for three years, and now they're going to shoot him for nothing."

Colonel Read shook his head sadly. "I know, Tim," he said. "I know. War is never fair. Who chooses which men get killed and which ones don't?" He touched my shoulder. "You have to accept it now. Be brave, and help your mother to bear up. She needs somebody now."

But I didn't feel brave nor like bearing up. All I felt was angry and bitter and ready to kill somebody. If I only knew who.

Sunday's church service seemed specially important so everybody could pray for the souls of the men who were going to die on Tuesday. Mother refused to go. Instead she sat calmly by the fire, sewing.

"We're required to go, Mother."

"I'm not going," she said. "They can murder who they like, church who they like, but I'm not going. For me the war is over."

I went. But after a half an hour of sitting in the balcony where I'd sat beside Sam so many hundreds of times, I began to cry, and I walked out. Nobody tried to stop me. I guess they knew how I felt.

We closed the tavern early that night. Nobody was there, anyway. I guess nobody wanted to be around us, it was too gloomy. "I would like to close the place forever," Mother said. I noticed that she had stopped drinking rum, for it was already over and there wasn't anything left to be nervous about.

"It was Father's tavern," I said.

"I won't serve any more Continental officers," she said. "Never again. Never."

I knew I wouldn't be able to sleep that night, and I didn't think Mother would either, so I threw some extra logs on the fire and pulled chairs up in front of it. "We've got to think of something, Mother."

"There's nothing," she said. "Let the dead bury the dead."

"He isn't dead yet, Mother. He's still alive."

"He's dead, Tim," she said. "He's dead as your father is."

"No," I said. I got up and took Father's bayonet down from the wall over the mantlepiece. Then I went out into the kitchen, took the steel out of the rack and began to whet the bayonet. Mother didn't get up, she didn't say anything. I worked over the bayonet a good long time until I had an edge on it that would slice through a man like a hot nail going through butter. Then I went out to the taproom and put on my coat.

Mother didn't lift her eyes from the flames snapping over the logs. "Going to get yourself killed, son?"

"I'm going to save my brother," I said.

"No, you're not," she said in a soft whispery kind of a voice. "No, you're going to get yourself killed. Well you might as well. Let's have it all done with at once. How does the old line go? Men must fight and women must weep, but you'll get no more tears from me. I've done my weeping for this war."

I stared at her. Then I turned and went out the door, buttoning up my coat.

There was plenty of moonlight. Shining on those fields of snow it was almost as bright as daylight. I didn't dare walk along the road; you never knew who could be coming along. This meant that I had to work my way through woodlots and along hedgerows across the pastures, where the snow had not been packed as hard as it was on the road. Fortunately it had begun to pack of its own weight, so that my feet sunk in only a few inches with each step. But it was funny; nothing seemed to bother me. I didn't feel tired or cold or worried. My head was sort of out of focus. I didn't have any plan. I knew I ought to think of one, but I couldn't really get my mind working. All I could do was just keep going on until I came to the encampment and then see what I did next.

Finally I came to the line of trees that ran along the ridge at the top of the encampment. I dropped into a crouch and slipped from tree to tree. There weren't many of them left: the soldiers had cut most of the wood for lumber and firewood. Then I came to the last tree, just over the edge of the ridge. I stopped and stared down. The ridge sloped down sharply for about a hundred yards. The line of huts ran along the bottom, with the muddy road alongside of them, and here and there a cannon or wagon standing. There were corrals for horses and livestock, but hardly any people. Light came out of the chinks and cracks in the buildings, making slashes and dots on the snow.

The stockade was dead in front of me. I stared at it —the little hut just like the others was surrounded by that ten-foot-high fence. There was a guard standing at the corner of the stockade, but he didn't seem to be too alert. I figured he'd be cold and thinking about getting warm and not keeping too close a watch around.

I still hadn't made any plan, but there didn't seem to be many choices. About the only thing I could do was slip down there, kill the guard, open the gate and let the prisoners out. And if he spotted me first, I could try to fling the bayonet over the fence and hope that Sam could get himself out in the confusion. It wasn't much of a plan, but it was the only one I could think of.

The trees had been cut off the hillside between me and the stockade, but there were plenty of stumps and boulders scattered all over it, and I figured if I was careful, I could slip down from one to the next until I reached the bottom. Down there was an empty space of fifty feet or so between the last stump and the stockade. I'd just have to make a dash for it. I figured that the snow there was bound to be packed down pretty hard— not bad for running.

I began to slip down the steep hillside from stump to boulder. I went mostly on hands and knees, getting pretty soaked in the snow. I kept an eye out on the guard. He didn't seem to be looking around much.

I was nearly at the bottom of the slope now, but I was still high enough on the hillside to see over the walls of the stockade. I stopped and stared. I couldn't see anybody moving around. The prisoners were all inside the hut, staying warm, I figured, although I didn't think they would be doing much sleeping. I wondered whether you cared about being warm if you knew you were going to die soon. I decided that you probably did.

I glanced at the guard. He still wasn't moving much, so I slipped the rest of the way down the hill behind some boulders, until I was at the edge of the open space of snow. The stockade was now only fifty feet away. I stared at the guard. He didn't move for several moments. He was leaning on his musket with his head bent forward, and I suddenly realized that he was asleep. I took the bayonet out of my belt and clutched it tight in my hand. If Sam could kill people, so could

I. I decided I would go for his throat if I could, so he wouldn't make any noise. I raised up a little. My heart was pounding, my breath was shallow and my hand was shaking.

Then I stood up and charged out from behind the boulder across the empty space of clear moonlight, my feet going crunch, crunch in the snow. The guard stirred. I drove my feet faster. He jerked his head up and stared at me, sort of dazed. I slammed forward. "Halt," he shouted. He swept the musket up, the bayonet pointing straight at me, twenty feet away.

I jerked to a stop. "Sam," I shouted, and "Sam," again as loud as I could. The guard lunged toward me. I lifted the bayonet and threw it into the air. It flashed in the moonlight, spinning lazily over and over and fell into the stockade. Then I turned and began racing as fast as I could across the snow for the safety of the boulders on the hillside. I had gone only three paces when the musket went off with a terrific roar. I felt something tug at my shoulder—no more than a tug— and I dashed onto the slope, and then began staggering upward, zigzagging from boulder to boulder to keep protection at my back. Behind me there was shouting and running and the sound of a horse being wheeled around. Another musket went off, and then another. I heard a ball smack into a stump somewhere near me. Now I was getting near the top. I struggled on, my breath rasping in my throat, and then I reached the trees at the top of the ridge and flung myself flat. They'd never get me now. They couldn't gallop horses in the snow fields, and I was too far ahead for them to catch me on foot. I rolled over and looked down. Two or three soldiers were starting to struggle up the slope. There were men running everywhere, and horses being saddled, and officers shouting.

I stared into the stockade. There was no action there, no people moving at all. Lying in the center of that square of snow, something shiny glistened in the moonlight. And I knew it had all been a waste. The prisoners weren't in the stockade anymore. They'd been moved to someplace else. I clutched my shoulder where it was bleeding a little, and started for home, running all the way.

Mother was asleep in her chair in front of the fire. Quietly I took off my shirt and looked at the wound. The ball had skipped right across the top of my left shoulder. A little chunk of flesh was gone. My arm felt numb, but nothing seemed to be broken. I washed the wound and dressed it, and then I hid the shirt with the bullet hole in it inside my mattress. I figured they might be able to guess who'd thrown that bayonet into the stockade, but nobody would be able to prove anything. I went to bed and fell asleep immediately.

Mother refused to go to the execution. I went. I

knew that Sam would want somebody there, and besides, somebody would have to claim the body. They had built a gallows up on a hill to the west of the encampment. A crowd had gathered around it. I waited down the road until a troop of soldiers came by. First came the drummers playing a slow roll, and then the troops and then Sam and Edward Jones riding in a cart. Their hands were tied behind their backs, and around their necks there were ropes that were tied to the cart, too. Behind them were more soldiers. General Putnam was going to make sure the troops saw the execution as an example. "Sam," I shouted as he went by.

He looked around at me. His face was dead white but he managed to give me a grin—not much of a one, but a grin. Then they passed on by. I waited until the last of the troops had gone through, then I ran up to where the crowd was standing and began to push my way through. When people saw who it was they let me pass. I pushed my way up near the front of the crowd, but not all the way. I had a funny feeling that I wanted to be hidden. I didn't want to stand out where people could see me.

They had already gotten Edward Jones upon the platform of the gallows. They had put a sack over his head. The rope dangled from the gallows an arm above. A soldier slipped the noose over his head. My eyes were misty and I couldn't see very well. Nathanial

Bartlett, the Presbyterian minister, stepped up onto the scaffold and said a prayer. Then he stepped away. I looked down at the ground. There was a funny thump and the crowd gasped. I looked up. Jones was hanging down below the scaffold at the end of the rope. His feet almost touched the ground and they were sort of dancing around.

I hadn't seen Sam, but now they brought him out from somewhere in a bunch of soldiers. They sort of shoved him into the empty space in front of the gallows. He had a sack over his head, too, and I wondered what it was like to be inside of that—was it hot and did it itch? Mr. Bartlett came out and said another prayer over Sam. I tried to pray myself, but my mouth was dry and I couldn't get the words out. They turned Sam sideways to the crowd. Three soldiers stepped in front of him and raised their muskets. They were so close the gun muzzles were almost touching Sam's clothes. I heard myself scream, "Don't shoot him, don't shoot him," and at that moment Sam slammed backwards as if he'd been knocked over by a mallet. I never heard the guns roar. He hit the ground on his belly and flopped over on his back. He wasn't dead yet. He lay there shaking and thrashing about, his knees jerking up and down. They had shot him from so close that his clothes were on fire. He went on jerking with flames on his chest until another soldier shot him again. Then he stopped jerking.

Epilogue

I HAVE WRITTEN THIS STORY DOWN IN THIS YEAR 1826, on the fiftieth anniversary of the founding of our nation, to commemorate the short life of my brother Samuel Meeker, who died forty-seven years ago in the service of his country. I am sixty-four. Although I hope to go on living in health for some time yet, the major portion of my own life is spent. It has been a happy life, and successful, for the most part.

I no longer live in Redding. After Sam's death I hated the place and wanted to go away; but the war went on for almost three more years, and while the fighting was on it was difficult to think of building a new life in another place.

For the first few months after Sam's death I was not able to do much more than my basic chores. But time heals wounds, and by the next fall I had become used to the ache in my heart, and I began to think about what I should do with my life. I started to make a study of calculating and surveying with Mr. Heron who was kind and didn't charge me for lessons. When the war finally ended Mother and I sold the tavern and moved out to Pennsylvania where new lands were opening up and surveyors were much in demand. After moving around a bit we finally settled in the town of Wilkes-Barre. We built a tavern there, and I began buying and selling land. With the profits from this activity I built a saw mill, and then a store to go along with the tavern, and then I joined with some other men to found a bank. I married and had children, and with work and God's will I prospered, so that I am able today to enjoy my children, my grandchildren, my orchards and my gardens in peace and comfort.

Mother never really got over Sam's death. She kept to her vow, and so long as the war went on she refused to serve Continental officers. I had to do it myself. She lived to a ripe old age and even at the end she would frequently speak of him in conversation or tell stories about his headstrong ways to my children. But she was tough in spirit, she survived to enjoy her grandchildren and her new life. She left her mark on the history of our country.

It will be, I am sure, a great history. Free of British domination, the nation has prospered and I along with it. Perhaps on some other anniversary of the United States somebody will read this and see what the cost has been. Father said, "In war the dead pay the debts of the living," and they have paid us well. But somehow, even fifty years later, I keep thinking that there might have been another way, beside war, to achieve the same end.

How much
of this book
is true?

Historians have a great many ways of finding out what happened in the past and why, but they cannot find out everything. In writing this book we have stuck to history as closely as we could, but of course we have had to make a good deal of it up. The town of Redding, Connecticut, is real, and existed in those days exactly as we have described it—at least insofar as we know. The house we have called the Meeker tavern is still there, at the southeast corner of the junction of Route 58 and Cross Highway. The church burned down and another was built on the site in 1833. In the churchyard you can find the gravestones of various members of the Heron and Meeker families.

General Putnam's Redding encampment is now known as Putnam Park. A few huts have been rebuilt to show how they were in the old days, and if you ever go there, you can see the slope where somebody might have slipped down from stump to stump, although today it is overgrown with trees again.

Many of the people were real, too. General Israel Putnam was a famous American patriot, the tough-minded, loyal, brave kind of man we have described him as. Colonel Read was also a real person, and did the sort of things we had him do in this book. Tom Warrups was real, and really lived in a hut such as we have described up behind Colonel Read's house. Ned, the slave, was real, and he died exactly as we have described it. William Heron was a real but somewhat mysterious figure in history. It appears that he was working for the Americans as well as the British. At the least he must have been a double agent, but historians are not sure exactly what role he played in the war. Captain Betts, Daniel Starr, Amos Rogers, little Jerry Sanford, the minister John Beach—these, too, were real people. And they lived and died just as we have told it here.

Of course the exact things that we have had these people do and say in this book are fictitious. We have tried to make them act as we believe they would have acted under these circumstances, but we are only guessing.

What about the Meekers? There was a Meeker family in Redding, who owned the mill down by the Aspectuck River, where Jerry and Tim went fishing for shad. You can find the spot near where Meeker Hill crosses the river. But we don't know much more about the Meekers than that. Essentially, we have made them up—Tim, Sam, and their mother and father. Betsy Read, too, we made up. We have been as careful as we could to make sure that they did the kinds of things they would have done in those days. However, we have used modern language in telling the story. Partly this was to make the story easier to read; but mainly it is because nobody is really sure how people talked in those days.

What about the story itself? The main historical incidents are all real, except of course for the part the Meeker family played in them. Yale students did rush away to get weapons and join the war in 1775. The Rebels did come through Redding and collect people's weapons, because Redding really was a strong Tory town. The trip across to Verplancks Point was invented, but Verplancks Point was real—you can visit the town